CliffsNotes™

King Lear

By Sheri Metzger, Ph.D.

IN THIS BOOK

- Learn about the Life and Background of the Playwright

Best-Selling

...es in

...tes

About the Author

Sheri Metzger currently teaches Literature and Composition in the University Honors Program and in the English Department at The University of New Mexico. Sheri has taught at UNM for the past ten years.

Publisher's Acknowledgments

Editorial

Project Editor: Alissa Cayton

Acquisitions Editor: Greg Tubach

Copy Editor: Linda Stark

Editorial Administrator: Michelle Hacker

Editorial Assistant: Laura Jefferson

Production

Indexer: York Production Services, Inc.

Proofreader: York Production Services, Inc.

Hungry Minds Indianapolis Production Services

CliffsNotes™ *King Lear*

Published by:

Hungry Minds, Inc.

909 Third Avenue

New York, NY 10022

www.hungryminds.com

www.cliffsnotes.com (CliffsNotes Web site)

Printed in the United States of America

10 9 8 7 6 5 4 3

1V/QR/QW/QQ/IN

Distributed in the United States by Hungry Minds, Inc.

Distributed by CDG Books Canada Inc. for Canada; by Transworld Publishers Limited in the United Kingdom; by IDG Norge Books for Norway; by IDG Sweden Books for Sweden; by IDG Books Australia Publishing Corporation Pty. Ltd. for Australia and New Zealand; by TransQuest Publishers Pte Ltd. for Singapore, Malaysia, Thailand, Indonesia, and Hong Kong; by Gotop Information Inc. for Taiwan; by ICG Muse, Inc. for Japan; by Norma Comunicaciones S.A. for Columbia; by Intersoft for South Africa; by Eyrolles for France; by International Thomson Publishing for Germany, Austria and Switzerland; by Distribuidora Cuspide for Argentina; by LR International for Brazil; by Galileo Libros for Chile; by Ediciones ZETA S.C.R. Ltda. for Peru; by WS Computer Publishing Corporation, Inc., for the Philippines; by Contemporanea de Ediciones for Venezuela; by Express Computer Distributors for the Caribbean and West Indies; by Micronesia Media Distributor, Inc. for Micronesia; by Grupo Editorial Norma S.A. for Guatemala; by Chips Computadoras S.A. de C.V. for Mexico; by Editorial Norma de Panama S.A. for Panama; by American Bookshops for Finland. Authorized Sales Agent: Anthony Rudkin Associates for the Middle East and North Africa.

For general information on Hungry Minds' products and services please contact our Customer Care department; within the U.S. at 800-762-2974, outside the U.S. at 317-572-3993 or fax 317-572-4002.

For sales inquiries and resellers information, including discounts, premium and bulk quantity sales and foreign language translations please contact our Customer Care department at 800-434-3422, fax 317-572-4002 or write to Hungry Minds, Inc., Attn: Customer Care department, 10475 Crosspoint Boulevard, Indianapolis, IN 46256.

For information on licensing foreign or domestic rights, please contact our Sub-Rights Customer Care department at 212-884-5000.

For information on using Hungry Minds' products and services in the classroom or for ordering examination copies, please contact our Educational Sales department at 800-434-2086 or fax 317-572-4005.

Please contact our Public Relations department at 212-884-5163 for press review copies or 212-884-5000 for author interviews and other publicity information or fax 212-884-5400.

For authorization to photocopy items for corporate, personal, or educational use, please contact Copyright Clearance Center, 222 Rosewood Drive, Danvers, MA 01923, or fax 978-750-4470.

Library of Congress Cataloging-in-Publication Data

Metzger, Sheri, 1984-

CliffNotes Shakespeare's King Lear / by Sheri Metzger

p. cm.

Includes bibiliographical refrences

ISBN 0-7645-8582-7 (alk. paper)

1. Shakespeare, William, 1564-1616. King Lear Examinations–Study guides. 2. Lear, King (Legendary character) 3. Kings and rulers in literature. 4. Tragedy. I. Title: Shakespeare's King Lear. II. Title: King Lear. III. Title

PR2819 .M48 2000

822.3'3--dc21   00-039690

CIP

Hungry Minds™ is a trademark of Hungry Minds, Inc.

Table of Contents

How to Use This Book

CliffsNotes *King Lear* supplements *The Arden Edition of the Words of William Shakespeare* (Routledge, reprinted 1989) edited by Kenneth Muir, giving you background information about the playwright, an introduction to the play, a graphical character map, critical commentaries, expanded glossaries, and a comprehensive index. CliffsNotes Review tests your comprehension of the original text and reinforces learning with questions and answers, practice projects, and more. For further information on Shakespeare and *King Lear,* check out the CliffsNotes Resource Center.

CliffsNotes provides the following icons to highlight essential elements of particular interest:

 Reveals the underlying themes in the work.

 Helps you to more easily relate to or discover the depth of a character.

 Uncovers elements such as setting, atmosphere, mystery, passion, violence, irony, symbolism, tragedy, foreshadowing, and satire.

 Enables you to appreciate the nuances of words and phrases.

Don't Miss Our Web Site

Discover classic literature as well as modern-day treasures by visiting the CliffsNotes Web site at www.cliffsnotes.com. You can obtain a quick download of a CliffsNotes title, purchase a title in print form, browse our catalog, or view online samples.

You'll also find interactive tools that are fun and informative, links to interesting Web sites, tips, articles, and additional resources to help you, not only for literature, but for test prep, finance, careers, computers, and the Internet too. See you at www.cliffsnotes.com!

LIFE AND BACKGROUND OF THE PLAYWRIGHT

Personal Background

Only a few documents chronicle William Shakespeare's life, and thus, scholars have been forced to attempt a reconstruction of the playwright's years based on whatever official records have survived. Shakespeare's father moved to Stratford-upon-Avon from nearby Snitterfield sometime before 1557, when he married Mary Arden, the daughter of a prosperous farmer. John Shakespeare was a leather worker and merchant, who held several posts in local government after he settled in Stratford. After the couple married, they had eight children. William Shakespeare was the third child and the first son born to the couple. His baptism was recorded April 26, 1564, and although the exact date of his birth is not known, it is now celebrated on April 23, which is also the day on which he died in 1616.

Education and Marriage

Shakespeare's education is a matter of speculation, because no school records have ever been found; likely, he attended the local grammar school, King's New School, which was free. Shakespeare probably began school at the age of 4 or 5, as most boys did, in a school affiliated with the grammar school. At age 7, he would have transferred to King's New School, which emphasized a liberal arts education. Shakespeare would have learned Latin while at this school, since the study of Latin was central to most Elizabethan education. His education ended after grammar school, and Shakespeare did not attend university.

In November 1582, an 18-year-old Shakespeare married 26-year-old Anne Hathaway. Their daughter Susanna was baptized six months later. On February 2, 1585, twins, Hamnet and Judith, were also baptized. Hamnet died at age 11, but both Susanna and Judith lived to be adults, marrying, and providing Shakespeare with grandchildren.

Career Highlights

There are no definitive records of Shakespeare's life between the birth of his twins in 1585 and reference to his stage success, noted in a letter dated 1592, but it is thought that he went to London sometime around 1587 or 1588. Records indicate that Shakespeare appeared as an actor and as a playwright. He also made money as shareholder in an acting company, The Lord Chamberlain's Men, and as such, he would have received a share of the gate receipts. But most actors and playwrights depended on patronage for their survival, and this was also true for Shakespeare. Eventually, Shakespeare became one of the owners of the Globe theatre, which was built in 1599. He later became an investor in the Blackfriars theatre, which opened in 1609. Shakespeare wrote many of his plays specifically for performance in these two theatres.

Literary Works

Shakespeare was very casual about the publication of his works, apparently having little interest in saving his writings. The 1623 Folio contains most of Shakespeare's plays, but they were not published in chronological order and do not include the dates of their original composition. Instead, the best scholars can do is to examine the Quarto editions, published during Shakespeare's life, or references from contemporary letters or diaries and try to determine from those dates the possible timeframe for a play's first performance. After careful research, scholars have assigned probable dates of composition to Shakespeare's work, and those dates, used by the editors of the *Oxford Shakespeare* and adopted by other editors, including the editors of the *Norton Shakespeare*, will be used in the following discussion of the texts' probable dates of composition. In general, the plays before 1600 were historics and romantic comedies. After 1600, tragedies became the focus of Shakespeare's work, while the problem-comedies, such as *Measure for Measure*, were darker in content, exploring serious social and moral problems.

The first play written by Shakespeare is thought to be *Two Gentlemen of Verona*, first published in the 1623 Folio, but thought to have been composed in 1590–1591. *The Taming of the Shrew* was also first published in the 1623 Folio, but may have been written in 1592 or earlier. Next was *The First Part of the Contention of the Two Famous Houses of York and Lancaster (The Second Part of Henry VI)*, probably composed about 1594, followed by *Richard Duke of York (3 Henry VI)*, first printed in 1595.

The first of Shakespeare's Latin plays followed; the revenge tragedy *Titus Andronicus* was first printed in 1594. *The First Part of Henry the Sixth* is often attributed to multiple authors and there are no printed editions prior to the 1623 Folio, but the play is thought to have been performed for the first time in 1594–1595. This is followed by *The Tragedy of King Richard the Third*, with a first printing in 1597, but probably first performed in 1592–1593.

Shakespeare turned to a different genre, and the long narrative poem *Venus and Adonis* was published in 1593, the first of Shakespeare's works to be published by Shakespeare. Plays belonged to theatre companies and were often printed irregularly, but the poet could publish his work without difficulty. This poem was followed by another long narrative poem, *The Rape of Lucrece*, first published in 1594. Although *The Comedy of Errors* was not published until 1623, it presumably was written much earlier and was first performed in 1594. *Love's Labour's Lost* followed in 1594–1595, to be followed by *Love's Labour's Won*, which survives only in a small fragment.

In 1600, *A Midsummer Night's Dream* was printed, but it may have been performed as early as 1595, which is also thought to be the date of the composition of *The Most Excellent and Lamentable Tragedy of Romeo and Juliet*, first published in 1597. Both plays offer contrasting views of love and marriage. *The Tragedy of King Richard the Second* follows, but this play, whose abdication scene was said to have been deleted during the lifetime of Elizabeth I, was not printed until 1597. Although it was not published until 1623, *The Life and Death of King John* is usually dated at about 1596. Because of its perceived anti-Semitic content, *The Merchant of Venice* has been surrounded in controversy, but when it was first registered in 1598, its content simply reflected accepted views.

Shakespeare turned once again to history for inspiration with the composition of *The History of Henry the Fourth (1 Henry IV)*, first printed in 1598. Comedy appeared next with the composition of *The Merry Wives of Windsor* in 1597–1598. Although not printed until 1600, Shakespeare probably wrote *The Second Part of Henry Fourth* immediately after he finished the first play in the sequence. But as he had done before, he penned a comedy after the historical play—this time, *Much Ado About Nothing*, probably composed in 1598, but soon followed by *The Life of Henry the Fifth* in 1599. Another history followed, but this time Shakespeare turned to early Roman history for inspiration. Although *The Tragedy of Julius Caesar* was not published until 1623, its composition is thought to be 1598–1599. With the composition of *As You Like It*, probably in 1599, Shakespeare recalls the influences of earlier pastoral poetry; however, this comedy marks the end of the playwright's light romantic comedies.

The year 1600 represents the beginning of a new phase in Shakespeare's compositions with the printing of *The Tragedy of Hamlet, Prince of Denmark*. *Twelfth Night, or What You Will* follows a year later and marks a move toward darker comedies, with plots and characters who are often cruel rather than comic. With *Troilus and Cressida* in 1601–1602, Shakespeare turns to Greek antiquity and *The Iliad* for inspiration, although as usual, Shakespeare rewrites the story to suit his needs. *Measure for Measure* is another of Shakespeare's dark comedies, not published until 1623 but first performed in 1604. During the same period (1603–1604), he was also writing *The Tragedy of Othello, The Moor of Venice* and *All's Well That Ends Well*, a complex comedy that raises questions about accepted gender roles. With *The Life of Timons of Athens*, Shakespeare again turns to history, but this play, as with several others, was first published in the 1623 Folio.

The History of King Lear or *The Tragedy of King Lear*, first printed in 1607—1608, exists in two different texts, and are thus often published on facing pages or combined in one text. The composition of *The Tragedy of Macbeth* follows and is usually dated at 1606. At the same time, Shakespeare was writing his sequel to *Julius Caesar, The Tragedy of Antony and Cleopatra*. *Pericles, Prince of Tyre*, probably 1607—1608, is thought to be a collaboration between Shakespeare and George Wilkins. With *Coriolanus* in 1608, Shakespeare again finds his source in Roman history.

After 1610, Shakespeare left London and returned to Stratford and semiretirement. But he continued to write plays, with *The Winter's Tale* (1609–1611), *Cymbeline, King of Britain* (1609–1610), and *The Tempest* (1611), largely composed in Stratford. Shakespeare's life as a playwright concluded with his creation of *All is True* or as it was also known, *The Famous History of the Life of Henry the Eighth* (1613), and *Two Noble Kinsmen* (1613–1614).

While writing his plays, Shakespeare was also composing sonnets, a format adapted by English poets from its Petrarchan origins. Although he probably began composing sonnets early in his writing career, evidence exists that Shakespeare continued revising his sonnets during the 1590s and through the early 1600s, finally publishing the entire sequence in 1609. The sonnet sequence was followed by "A Lover's Complaint," but probably composed earlier, as well (1602–1605) and a collection of occasional poems.

Although Shakespeare's authorship has been questioned, the man, as a playwright, was quite well known in Elizabethan London. A conspiracy to disguise the writer's true identity would have been difficult to sustain. In the end, it really does not matter whether the man we know as William Shakespeare composed the plays attributed to him or not. The plays exist for our enjoyment, and that is sufficient.

INTRODUCTION TO THE PLAY

Introduction

King Lear was first printed in 1608. This initial printing is now referred to as the First Quarto. Another Quarto version was printed in 1619, and *King Lear* appeared again in a 1623 Folio edition. The First Quarto contains 300 lines not found in the Folio, and the Folio contains 100 lines not found in the First Quarto. Because many differences exist between the Quarto and Folio editions, some recent anthologies of Shakespeare's works contain play text from both editions, and may also include a conflated edition derived from a combination of both the First Quarto and Folio versions.

Although the text was not printed until 1608, the play was performed in December 1606. The exact date of composition is not known, so scholars often try to base the point in time on references in the play itself. Because of this uncertainty and the textual references, the composition of *King Lear* may have taken place anywhere from 1604 to 1606.

The story of King Lear and his daughters was a familiar tale in Elizabethan England, where it was generally believed to be based on historical fact, having been taken from ancient British history. A legal case of the times also may be due credit for contributing to the drama. In an act that generated extensive publicity, two daughters attempted to have their father declared insane so that they might seize his estate. The younger daughter, Cordell, objected.

This similarity of name and plot might have sparked some interest in resurrecting a familiar plot. However, accounts of King Lear surface in several texts; so, Shakespeare may have turned to other sources as well in exploring this ancient story.

Lear's story appears in Geoffrey of Monmouth's *Historia Regum Britanniae*, published about 1135. This text includes insights into the kings of the ancient, pre-Christian Britain. Years later, Lear's story is repeated in Raphael Holinshed's 1577 book, *Chronicles of England*, which includes an ending in which Cordelia and Lear both survive her sisters' treachery. Cordelia succeeds her father to the throne, upon his death; but she is later imprisoned and commits suicide. The John Higgens 1574 edition of *Mirror for Magistrates* introduces the name of Albany and includes a story of Cordelia, in which she commits suicide—something that does not occur in the older play. The Lear story is also retold in Edmund Spenser's 1590 epic poem, *The Faerie Queene*, where

Cordelia commits suicide by hanging. The Gloucester plot may have been taken from Sir Philip Sidney's 1590 poem, *Arcadia*, in which an old prince is blinded by his illegitimate son, but is ultimately saved by his legitimate son. Much of the events that occur to Gloucester are derived from this source.

The True Chronicle of King Leir is first entered into the Stationers's register in 1594, although there is no record of its publication until the 1605 edition appears. This source, while containing the basic Lear story, is grounded in Christianity, something not contained in the story of the ancient Leir or in Shakespeare's Lear. Many scholars do find ample evidence of Christian ideology in *King Lear*, but no overt emphasis on Christianity, as there is in Shakespeare's principle source. The old play has a happy ending, where evil is punished and good is rewarded, thus reinforcing the Christian belief in divine justice. Instead of proposing such easy answers, Shakespeare leaves his audience to ponder the role of God and divine justice. As he did so often in borrowing from sources, Shakespeare wove threads of historical accounts and original writings to create the fabric of his own *King Lear*.

Historical Context

By the time Shakespeare was writing *King Lear*, the English had survived years of civil war and political and religious upheaval. Considerable turmoil followed the death of Henry VIII, and under his oldest daughter's rule (Mary I), the country experienced both civil and religious chaos, with the conflict between Catholicism and the Church of England resulting in much bloodshed.

After Mary's death, Elizabeth I assumed the throne, leading to a period of extended peace. In spite of their contentment with Elizabeth's rule, the populace worried significantly about England's future because Elizabeth was unmarried, and she refused to select a possible heir. No citizen wanted a repeat of the events that marked the earlier transfer of power. Thus, the lack of an heir created fears about a possible successor to her throne, which were finally resolved in 1603 when Elizabeth appointed James IV of Scotland to be her heir, and eventually, the new king of England.

The English understood that a strong country needed an effective leader to protect it from potential invasion. Elizabeth's powerful leadership had saved England when the Spanish attempted an invasion in

1588, and much of the credit for her success was attributed to her earlier efforts to unite England and to end the dissention that was destroying the country. No ruler would have deliberately chosen to divide a kingdom, not after having witnessed the conflicts that had marked England's recent history. The division of a country would have weakened it, leading to squabbles between petty lords and the absence of an effective central government, and thus, the absence of an effective defense. After this long period of uncertainty, Shakespeare's Elizabethan audience would have been horrified at Lear's choice to divide his kingdom and so, create disunity.

Structure of the Play

Shakespeare's *King Lear* is a five-act tragedy. Most Elizabethan theatre adheres to the five-act structure, which corresponds to divisions in the action. The first act is the Exposition, in which the playwright sets forth the problem and introduces the main characters.

In *King Lear*, Act I establishes the nature of the conflict between Cordelia and Lear, among Goneril and Regan and Lear, and between Gloucester and Edgar. This first act also establishes the duplicitous, or treacherously twofold, nature of Goneril, Regan, and Edmund, while demonstrating that Cordelia and Edgar are good characters. The remainder of the play's central characters also make an appearance in this act.

Act II is the Complication, in which the entanglement or conflict develops further. The erosion of Lear's power begins, the depth of the conflict between Lear and his daughters is revealed, and the conspiracy that unites Goneril, Regan, and Edmund is established.

Act III is the Climax; and as the name suggests, this is when the action takes a turning point and the crisis occurs. In this act, Lear has been cast adrift in the storm, and his words reveal that his mind is also now lost. Likewise, the extent of Regan and Cornwall's depravity is revealed as they torture Gloucester, ultimately gouging out his eyes.

Act IV is called the Falling Action, which signals the beginning of the play's resolution. In this act, Edgar reunites with his father, although Gloucester is still unaware that Edgar is his son, and Cordelia returns to Lear, who begins to emerge from his madness. In action that indicates the approaching downfall of the conspirators, Cornwall's death is revealed, and Edgar kills Oswald. The audience sees in Act IV the tragedy overtaking the hero, as well as the efforts in progress to aid the hero.

Act V is called the Catastrophe, wherein the conclusion occurs. As the name suggests, this act brings closure to the play, a resolution to the conflict, and death to the hero. As the play draws to a close, Regan and Goneril die, Edmund is killed in a duel with his brother, Lear and Cordelia die, and Edgar is chosen to restore peace to the kingdom.

Literary Devices

Students of Shakespeare's plays quickly come to appreciate the literary devices that the playwright employs in constructing his tragedy. For example, most Shakespearean tragedy contains elements of comic relief, designed to provide a sort of catharsis, a chance for the audience to "catch its breath." But in this case, no comic relief relieves the tension as Lear plays out the drama that his decision has set in motion. Characters, who in other tragedies might contain comedic elements— such as the Fool—are far removed from comedy. The Fool's purpose is to make Lear laugh, but instead, he functions largely as a Greek Chorus, commenting on the action and pointing out to Lear subtleties of his behavior and dangers that he faces. But his compassion, tinged with sarcasm, is never funny.

Shakespeare also uses soliloquy as an important literary device in his plays. Most Shakespearean tragedies contain soliloquies, because they offer a way for the playwright to divulge a character's inner thoughts. The soliloquy requires that the character must think that he is alone on stage, as he reveals what he is thinking for the benefit of the audience. *King Lear* contains eleven soliloquies, with Edmund using this device most often to explain his plotting to the audience. Edgar also uses this device several times, most notably when he explains the reasons he will henceforth be known as Tom. A soliloquy is different from a monologue, in which a character speaks aloud his thoughts, but with other characters present. Shakespeare also frequently employs the aside, in which the character addresses the audience, but other characters are not supposed to hear. The aside allows the audience to learn details that most of the characters on stage do not know. For example, Goneril uses an aside to reveal that she has poisoned Regan.

The double plot is another important literary device in this play. King Lear is the only Shakespearean tragedy to employ two similar plots, each functioning in an almost exact parallel manner. With two plots, perfectly intertwined and yet offering parallel lessons, Shakespeare is able to demonstrate the tragic consequences that result when man's law is given precedence over natural law. Eventually, Gloucester and Lear learn the importance of natural law with both finally turning to nature to find answers for why their children have betrayed them. Their counterparts, Edmund, Goneril, Regan, and Cornwall, represent the evil that functions in violation of natural law.

The double plot serves an important function, emphasizing natural law as an essential facet of both plots. Shakespeare then uses the two plots to point to how essential an acknowledgment of natural law is in a moral society. In both plots, the absence of natural law is destructive, and ultimately even those who are good cannot act to save Cordelia or the other good characters from the ravages of evil and tyranny.

Shakespeare's use of doubling appears throughout *King Lear*. For example, Kent's true loyalty to the king is paralleled by Oswald's corrupt loyalty to Goneril. Lear also has two sons-in-law. Regan's husband is the cruel Cornwall, whose only interest is in furthering his own ambitions. He has no real interest in the well-being of the kingdom, and sacrificing Lear is an acceptable price to pay to gain the power he desires. Cornwall's parallel is Goneril's husband, Albany, who has no personal ambitions or thoughts of personal glory. Albany's goal is to preserve the kingdom and save Lear's life.

Still another set of doubles is France and Burgundy, whose response to Cordelia's loss of dowry differs in drastic ways. Where Burgundy has no use for a Cordelia who lacks money, land, and rank, France is willing to take Cordelia, even if she has no material possessions. Thus, France who sees Cordelia as representing the greatest riches that her father possesses, is a contrasting double for the self-serving Burgundy.

Shakespeare wrote most of this play in verse, using iambic pentameter, which sometimes intimidates the playwright's audiences. Iambic pentameter is a literary term that defines the play's meter and the stresses placed on each syllable. In iambic pentameter, each complete line contains ten syllables, with each pair of syllables containing both an accented syllable and an unaccented syllable. Many Renaissance poets used iambic pentameter because the alternating stresses create a rhythm that contributes to the beauty of the play's language. Shakespeare also includes prose passages in his plays, with prose lines being spoken by characters of lower social rank. In *King Lear*, Edgar speaks prose when he is disguised as Tom; when he reemerges as Edgar, he resumes speaking in verse.

A Shakespearean glossary can help in understanding the language, but the biggest assist comes with practice. Reading and listening to Shakespeare's words becomes easier with repeated exposure. Reading aloud also helps in becoming familiar with Early Modern English. Over time, the unfamiliar language and the rhetorical devices that Shakespeare employs in writing his texts will cease to be strange, and the language will assume the beauty that was always hidden within it.

A Brief Synopsis

King Lear opens with a conversation between the earls of Kent and Gloucester, in which the audience learns that Gloucester has two sons: Edgar, who is his legitimate heir, and Edmund, his younger illegitimate son. This information will provide the secondary or subplot. Next, King Lear enters to state that he intends to remove himself from life's duties and concerns. Pointing at a map, Lear tells those in attendance that he has divided his kingdom into three shares, to be parceled out to his three daughters, as determined by their protestations of love. The two elder daughters, Goneril and Regan, exaggerate their love by telling their father that their affection for him exceeds all reasonable expectations. The youngest daughter, Cordelia, tells Lear that she loves him, but only as a daughter should love a father. Lear, angry and disappointed at what he deems a lack of devotion on Cordelia's part, divides his kingdom equally between Goneril and Regan, and banishes Cordelia. Later, France agrees to marry the now dowerless and banished Cordelia. When Kent attempts to defend Cordelia, Lear banishes him as well. Meanwhile, Goneril and Regan decide that if Lear becomes too much of a nuisance, they will have to decide what disciplinary actions to take.

In the developing subplot, Edmund complains of his unhappiness at being an illegitimate—and thus, disinherited—son. As part of his plot to claim what is not his, Edmund gives a false letter to his father, Gloucester, declaring that Edgar is proposing that they kill their father and split the wealth between them. The cunning Edmund easily convinces his father that Edgar cannot be trusted.

Within a short time, Lear moves to Goneril's palace. Goneril tells Lear that he needs a smaller troop, more decorous in behavior and better suited to the king's rank and age. The king is very angry and says he will pack up his people and move to Regan's palace. Lear's anger continues to build, and he calls upon nature to curse Goneril's womb. In response, Goneril turns out 50 of Lear's retinue.

As the subplot develops, Edmund wounds himself slightly, pretending that Edgar has attacked him. Certain that Edgar will also try to kill him, Gloucester promises to find the means to make Edmund his heir. After his escape into the woods, Edgar decides that he will disguise himself as a Bedlam beggar, who will be known as Poor Tom. Meanwhile, Cornwall orders an impassioned Kent placed in the stocks. Lear arrives and quickly realizes that Regan has joined Goneril in seeking to reduce Lear's authority. Lear reminds his daughters that he gave them all that they now enjoy, but they are unmoved. An angry Lear calls for his horse, and rides into the storm with his Fool for protection. Exposed to the storm, the Fool attempts to reason with his king, but Lear will have no part of submission, especially before his daughters. Soon the king and Fool are joined by Edgar disguised as Poor Tom.

Gloucester tells Edmund of the plot to save the king, unaware that he is divulging the plans to a traitor. Edmund immediately resolves to tell Cornwall of the plan. Edmund soon receives his reward: Gloucester's title and lands. The captured Gloucester is tortured by Regan, who fiendishly plucks at his beard, and Cornwall, who gouges out Gloucester's eyes, but not before one of Cornwall's servants draws a sword and stabs Cornwall, who soon dies of his wounds.

Later, Edgar is both shocked and dismayed when a blinded Gloucester is led in by one of his tenants. The disguised Edgar agrees to take Gloucester to the cliff he seeks, where he dupes Gloucester into thinking that he is at the edge of a precipice. After Gloucester jumps and loses consciousness, Edgar easily convinces his father that he has somehow survived a fall from the cliffs. Oswald arrives and attempts to kill Gloucester but is, instead, slain by Edgar. As he lays dying, Oswald gives Edgar a letter from Goneril instructing Edmund to murder Albany so that she will be free to wed Edmund.

Goneril and Edmund soon learn that Albany is a changed man, one who is pleased to learn of the proposed invasion by France and displeased when he learns that Gloucester has been replaced by his younger son, Edmund. Meanwhile, Cordelia learns of her father's deteriorated mental condition and returns to England with an army to defend her father. Within a short time, Cordelia and her father reunite.

In spite of Albany's intent to save Lear and Cordelia's lives, Edmund resolves that they will die. Edmund orders that Lear and Cordelia be imprisoned. Albany, Goneril, and Regan join Edmund, and a confrontation erupts among all four characters. Edmund's treachery is revealed, and he is wounded in a fight with Edgar, whom Edmund does not recognize as his brother. Soon, Regan dies, poisoned by Goneril, who then kills herself. Since he is now dying, Edmund admits that the charges against him are truthful, and he seeks to know the identity of his killer. Edgar confesses his lineage as brother and shares the news that their father, Gloucester, has died.

Edmund, who says he wants some good to come from so much death, reveals his and Goneril's plan to have both Lear and Cordelia murdered and to have Cordelia's death appear a suicide. Efforts to rescind these orders are too late, and soon Lear enters with a dead Cordelia in his arms. Unable to accept Cordelia's death, the king also dies, his body covering that of his youngest daughter. Albany informs Kent and Edgar that they must now rule the kingdom together, but Kent replies that he will soon leave the world to join his master. Edgar is left to speak of the sad weight of these events, which everyone must now endure.

List of Characters

King Lear King of Britain. Lear is the protagonist whose willingness to believe empty flattery leads to the deaths of many people.

Goneril Lear's eldest daughter who, after professing her deep love for her father, betrays him and plots his murder.

Regan Lear's second daughter. Regan joins forces with Goneril to destroy their father. Regan initially appears less harsh than her elder sister, but in the end, she proves to be as blood-thirsty as Goneril.

Cordelia Lear's youngest daughter. Cordelia genuinely loves her father, but her refusal to flatter him leads to her tragic death.

Fool Loyal member of the king's court. The Fool assumes the role of protector to Lear when Cordelia is banished.

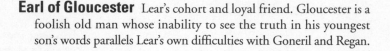

Earl of Gloucester Lear's cohort and loyal friend. Gloucester is a foolish old man whose inability to see the truth in his youngest son's words parallels Lear's own difficulties with Goneril and Regan.

Earl of Kent / Caius Lear's loyal friend and supporter. Although banished, Kent disguises himself as Caius in an effort to stay close to his king.

Edgar / Poor Tom Gloucester's older son. Edgar is Gloucester's only legitimate heir, but he must flee and hide from his father, disguised as Poor Tom, when he comes under suspicion.

Edmund Gloucester's younger, illegitimate, son. He is an opportunist whose ambitions lead him to form a union with Goneril and Regan.

Duke of Albany Goneril's husband. Albany grows in stature during the play and ultimately finds the strength to resist his wife's efforts to have Lear killed.

Duke of Cornwall Regan's brutal husband. Cornwall is vicious and savage as he tries to eliminate Lear and Gloucester.

Oswald Goneril's steward. Oswald is a willing accomplice to Goneril's plotting and proves a foil to Kent's devotion to Lear.

King of France Marries Cordelia. France is honorable and willing to support Cordelia's efforts to rescue her father.

Duke of Burgundy Suitor for Cordelia. Burgundy rejects Cordelia when he discovers that she will bring him no dowry.

Curan Gloucester's servant.

Old Man Tenant of Gloucester.

Servants to Cornwall Cornwall's retainers, who attack him in defense of Gloucester.

Doctor Attendant to Cordelia.

Character Map

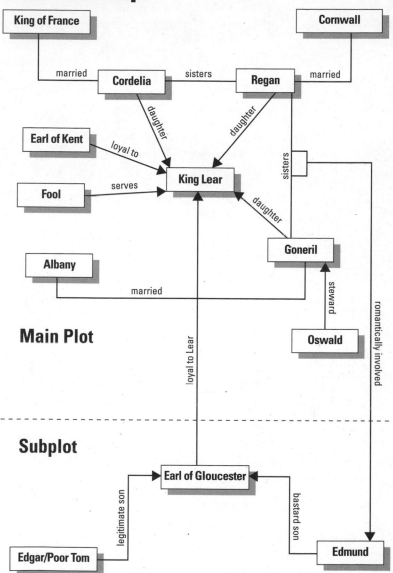

King of France — married — **Cordelia** — sisters — **Regan** — married — **Cornwall**

Cordelia — daughter → **King Lear**

Regan — daughter → King Lear

Earl of Kent — loyal to → King Lear

Fool — serves → King Lear

Regan — sisters — **Goneril**

Goneril — daughter → King Lear

Albany — married —

Oswald — steward → Goneril

romantically involved

Main Plot

loyal to Lear

- -

Subplot

Earl of Gloucester

Edgar/Poor Tom — legitimate son → Earl of Gloucester

Edmund — bastard son → Earl of Gloucester

CRITICAL COMMENTARIES

Act I
Scene 1

Summary

The scene opens in King Lear's palace. A conversation between Kent, Gloucester, and Gloucester's son Edmund introduces the play's primary plot: The king is planning to divide his kingdom among his three daughters. The audience also learns that Gloucester has two sons. The older, Edgar, is his legitimate heir, and the younger, Edmund, is illegitimate; however, Gloucester loves both sons equally. This information provides the subplot.

King Lear enters to a fanfare of trumpets, followed by his two sons-in-law—Albany and Cornwall—and his three daughters—Goneril, Regan, and Cordelia. Lear announces that he has divided his kingdom into three shares to be given to his daughters as determined by their declarations of love for him. Goneril, as the eldest, speaks first. She tells her father that her love for him is boundless. Regan, as the middle child, speaks next. Her love, she says, is even greater than Goneril's.

Finally, it is Cordelia's turn to express the depth of her love for her royal father. But when queried by Lear, Cordelia replies that she loves him as a daughter should love a father, no more and no less. She reminds her father that she also will owe devotion to a husband when she marries, and therefore cannot honestly tender all her love toward her father. Lear sees Cordelia's reply as rejection; in turn, he disowns Cordelia, saying that she will now be "a stranger to my heart and me" (I.1.114). King Lear then divides his kingdom between Goneril and Regan, giving each an equal share.

Kent interferes by asking Lear to reconsider his rash action. Lear is not swayed, and in anger, he banishes Kent for defending Cordelia and for confronting the king.

At Kent's departure, the King of France and Duke of Burgundy enter, both of whom are suitors for Cordelia's hand in marriage. They are told that Cordelia will not receive a dowry or inheritance from her father. The Duke withdraws his suit, because a wife without a dowry is of no use to him. In contrast, the King of France claims that Cordelia is a prize, even without her share of Lear's kingdom, and announces his intent to marry Cordelia.

Cordelia bids her sisters farewell, and leaves with the King of France. When Goneril and Regan are left alone, the two sisters reveal their plan to discredit the king.

Commentary

The play opens with a scene that introduces most of the primary characters and establishes both the main plot and a subplot. This first scene also is important because it provides the audience with an introduction to the character of Kent before he is banished and before he reappears disguised as Caius in Scene 4.

Character Insight

In the opening conversation, Gloucester speaks of Edmund's illegitimate birth in what can be described aptly as Elizabethan locker-room talk. Although Gloucester loves his illegitimate son Edmund and his legitimate son Edgar equally, Elizabethan society does not regard the two men as equals. Edmund realizes that his chances of a prosperous future are limited because he was born second to Gloucester from an unholy union. Edmund will not receive an equal inheritance under laws of primogeniture, which name the eldest son heir to his father's possessions. Gloucester relates to Kent that Edmund has been away seeking his fortune, but now he has returned—perhaps believing that he can find his fortune at home.

Initially, Lear appears to be a strong ruler, a monarch who has decided to divide his kingdom. Lear's choice will provide one clear benefit: Albany and Cornwall will be in charge of the outlying areas of his kingdom, which have not been easily governed. Lear plans to place Cordelia, with himself as her guest, in the center section. Lear recognizes that he is growing older and explains his decision to divide his kingdom by saying:

> 'tis our fast intent
> To shake all cares and business from our age,
> Conferring them on younger strengths, while we
> Unburden'd crawl toward death. (I.1.37–40)

But the one benefit derived from this division creates many problems. By delegating his royal authority to his daughters, Lear creates chaos within his family and his kingdom not unlike the civil distress experienced by Shakespeare's audience. At the time Shakespeare penned *King Lear*, the English had survived years of civil war and division. Thus, Shakespeare's Elizabethan audience would have been horrified at Lear's decision to divide his kingdom. The audience also would have questioned Shakespeare's inclusion of the French suitor, especially since Lear intends for Cordelia and her new husband to oversee the choice center section of his kingdom.

The fear that a foreign king might weaken England (and a Catholic monarch made it worse) would have made Lear's actions seem even more irresponsible to the audience. But Lear is doing more than creating political and social chaos; he is also giving his daughters complete responsibility for his happiness, and he will blame them later when he is not happy.

Moreover, the test that Lear devises to measure his daughters' love is a huge mistake. Lear is depicted as a wise ruler—he has, after all, held the country together successfully for many years. Yet he lacks the common sense or the ability to detect his older daughters' falseness. This flaw in Lear leads the audience to think him either mad or stupid.

The love test is derived from Shakespeare's source and so it is included. Shakespeare's primary source is an anonymous play, *The True Chronicle History of King Leir*, in which the love test is used to trick Cordelia into marriage. Consequently, the test of love is only a device to further the plot, which Shakespeare plucked from his source. It is important to remember that *King Lear* is not historically based, although sources state that the story was based on events occurring at about 800 B.C. *King Lear* should more accurately be regarded as a sort of fairy tale. In many ways, Goneril and Regan are similar to Cinderella's evil older sisters.

Goneril and Regan's expressions of love are so extreme that they are questionable as rational responses to Lear's test. Cordelia's reply is honest, but Lear cannot recognize honesty amid the flattery, which he craves. Of course, Lear is not being honest either when he asks Cordelia, "what can you say to draw / A third more opulent than your sisters?" (I.1.84–85). Lear plans to reward Cordelia's expected exaltation with a larger portion of his kingdom than that allotted to her sisters. The shares should be equal, but Lear clearly loves Cordelia more. Cordelia's reply, "Nothing," is a word that will reappear throughout the play—with disastrous connotations. "Nothing" is a key word that is repeated several times in the play, thus emphasizing the word's importance. Cordelia's uttering of "nothing" is echoed at the end of the play when she is dead, and "nothing" remains of her. But it is also important to remember that Lear really understands "nothing" about his daughters, just as Gloucester knows "nothing" about his sons. When Gloucester sees "nothing," he is finally able to see the truth, and when Lear emerges from the "nothingness" of his mental decline, it is to finally know that Cordelia has always loved him.

Theme

Cordelia loves Lear according to the bonds of a blood relationship, as paternity demands. Her response is in keeping with Elizabethan social norms, which expect a daughter to love her father because that is the law of nature. According to nature, man is part of a hierarchy, from God to king to father to child. The love between each of these parties is reciprocal, and Cordelia's love for her father is what she owes him.

Cordelia tempers her love test reply with reason—a simple, unembellished statement of the honor due a father from his daughter. Lear irrationally responds by denying Cordelia all affection and paternal care.

Character Insight

Kent's interference on Cordelia's behalf leads to another outburst from Lear. Like Cordelia, Kent is honest with the king, providing a voice of reason. Kent sees Lear making a mistake and tells him so. The depth of Lear's anger toward Kent suggests excessive pride—Lear cannot be wrong. Cordelia's answer injures Lear's pride; he needs her excessive protestations of love to justify giving her the choicer parcel of land. Lear's intense anger toward Kent also suggests the fragility of the king's emotional state.

Cordelia's two suitors provide more drama in this initial scene. The Duke of Burgundy cannot love Cordelia without her dowry, but the King of France points out that she is a prize as great as any dowry and correctly recognizes that Burgundy is guilty of selfish self-interest. France's reply to Cordelia reveals that he is, indeed, worthy of Cordelia's love:

> Fairest Cordelia, that art most rich, being poor,
> Most choice, forsaken, and most lov'd, despis'd!
> Thee and thy virtues here I seize upon,
> Be it lawful I take up what's cast away. (I.1.249–252)

The final section of this scene reveals that Cordelia knows that her sisters are liars, and so informs the audience of their dishonesty. Goneril replies that Cordelia deserves to be banished. This heated exchange foreshadows the feud that develops over the course of the next acts. Additional foreshadowing is supplied by Goneril and Regan's promise that if Lear becomes too much of a nuisance, they will have to deal with him accordingly. The first scene ends with Regan acknowledging that Lear isn't just weak because of old age, but that he has never really known himself—or his daughters. Regan's complaint reveals much about the relationship that Lear has with his daughters. His obvious preference for Cordelia has come at the expense of losing touch with his older daughters. Lear cannot recognize Goneril and Regan's deceit because he does not know them well enough to recognize when they are being dishonest. Lear's privileging of Cordelia prevents him from forming the kind of relationship with his older daughters that might have resulted in genuine love.

Scene 1 establishes a plot and subplot that will focus on a set of fathers and their relationships with their children. The audience will be privy to the conflict between father and child, and to fathers easily fooled by their children. Each father demonstrates poor judgment by rejecting a good child and trusting a dishonest child(ren). The actions that follow illustrate just how correct Regan's words will prove to be. It will soon be obvious how little Lear knows and understands his daughters as Goneril and Regan move to restrict both the size of his retinue and his power.

Glossary

Here and in the following glossary sections, difficult words and phrases are explained.

moiety 1. a half; either of two equal, or more or less equal, parts. 2. an indefinite share or part.

braz'd 1. made of, or coated with, brass or a brasslike substance. 2. made hard like brass.

proper fine; good; handsome.

wide-skirted vast; extensive.

felicitate made happy.

propinquity nearness of relationship; kinship.

make from to stay away from; avoid.

recreant failing to keep faith; disloyal; traitorous; apostate.

unpriz'd precious to be unimportant to one person, but appreciated or valued highly by another.

long-engrafted firmly established.

Act I
Scene 2

Summary

Edmund enters the scene—set in the Earl of Gloucester's house—talking out loud to himself. In this soliloquy, Edmund figuratively asks Nature why society sees him as inferior to his brother Edgar simply because he is not his father's legitimate firstborn. Edmund's soliloquy reveals his plan to undermine his brother's position by tricking his father with a forged letter, which he presents to Gloucester in this scene.

Edmund also succeeds in convincing Edgar that he's looking out for his brother's safety when he suggests that Edgar carry a weapon as protection from their father's anger—a wrath, Edmund intimates, that's directed toward Edmund.

Commentary

Character Insight

Edmund's musings offer insight into his unhappiness. Edmund feels that each brother, equally loved, should share equally in his father's bounty. But there is no equality under the current law, and Edmund's ideal is not reality. Edmund asks why he is not as respected as his brother:

> When my dimensions are as well compact,
> My mind as generous, and my shape as true,
> An honest madam's issue? Why brand they us
> With base? With baseness? Bastardy? Base, base? (I.2.7–10)

Theme

Edmund rejects the laws of state and society in favor of the laws he sees as eminently more practical and useful—the laws of superior cunning and strength. Edmund's willingness to seize what he wants invokes laws of nature, although not the natural laws familiar to Elizabethan audiences in a class-defined society. Instead, Edmund supports survival of the fittest, an animalistic nature not based on human morality and common decency. Edmund says that he will take what he deserves through wit, even if he is not entitled by birth. This resolve is an affront to the nature that Edgar addresses in his opening soliloquy; underestimating the force of nature will also prove critical to Edmund's downfall.

Character Insight

Edmund appears to be a villain without a conscience, selfishly driven to secure his own needs. Still, Edmund lacks the ill will of another of Shakespeare's villains, Iago, with whom Edmund is most often compared. In *Othello*, Iago acts without clear reason, since none of his suggested motives withstand a close examination. In contrast, Edmund has solid economic and emotional reasons for his actions. Edmund may also have overheard his father describe the "good sport at his making" (I.1.22). If so, Edmund's actions reveal a desire for personal revenge.

The cavalier attitude with which Gloucester dismisses Edmund's paternity further reinforces the difference between Edmund and Edgar. Where Edgar is entitled to his father's name, his title, and his property, Edmund is entitled to nothing but the coarse jesting that accompanied his conception.

Gloucester ignores any possibility that his youngest son may resent this easy dismissal of both Edmund's birth and his future prospects, but Edmund finds in his father's thoughtless words a reason to destroy Gloucester. In plotting his revenge, Edmund reveals that he is a worthy opponent, even though much of his desire for revenge is an emotional response to Gloucester's words. In Shakespeare's *Othello,* Iago makes sport of his actions while proving himself superior intellectually to those around him. In comparison, Edmund reacts to his situation with seriousness and reason, but his actions never stem from a need to make sport.

Style & Language

Language is particularly noteworthy in this scene. Shakespeare weaves in much talk of seeing, although Gloucester does not truly see until he is blinded later in the play. Gloucester says that if Edmund's letter contains nothing significant, then "I shall not need my spectacles" (I.2.35). But, of course, even with spectacles, he cannot see that Edmund is deceiving him. After exclaiming "let's see, let's see" (I.2.42), he shows that he can neither recognize the dishonestly in what he reads nor see that Edmund is lying. In mistaking Edmund's motives, Gloucester is already blind to the evil events unfolding around him.

Edmund condemns his father's age in the forged letter by suggesting that old men should step down and give control to those who are younger. Gloucester is referred to as an aged tyrant who desires to maintain control in order to keep his sons from receiving their inheritances.

This brief exchange reminds the audience of Goneril and Regan's dismissal of Lear's actions as those of an old man, unable to decipher or understand the actions around him. And just as Lear condemned the guiltless Cordelia, Gloucester now condemns the innocent Edgar, who has no knowledge of the false letter. The irony of the letter's message—that the old should be displaced—proves true for Gloucester. Clearly, he is not intuitive or quick enough to understand the plotting or undercurrents present around him. Gloucester buys into Edmund's trickery.

Gloucester asserts that the sun and moon play a role in current events. Gloucester absolves himself of any responsibility for his actions by giving power to the stars. Relying on astrological signs makes it easier to accept that Edgar might betray his father: "These late eclipses in the sun and moon portend no good to us" (I.2.100–101). This reflection echoes Lear's earlier statement about the astrological influences on man's life: "By all the operation of the orbs / From whom we do exist and cease to be" (I.1.110–111). Both fathers count on the stars to provide an excuse for their children's actions. But Edmund has his own opinion of these astrological signs, of which he says:

This is the excellent foppery of the world, that, when we are sick in fortune, often the surfeits of our own behaviour, we make guilty of our disasters the sun, the moon, and stars; as if we were villains on necessity, fools by heavenly compulsion, knaves, thieves, and teachers by spherical predominance, drunkards, liars and adulterers by an enforc'd obedience of planetary influence; and all that we are evil in, by a divine thrusting on. An admirable evasion of whoremaster man, to lay his goatish disposition to the charge of a star! (I.2.115–125)

Edmund acknowledges that man is ultimately responsible for his actions. This passage also reveals how effectively Edmund is able to work the audience. He succeeds in making his father's beliefs and actions appear foolish. Gloucester's reliance on the stars appears to support Edmund's contention that his father is a witless old man.

Edmund also easily fools Edgar, but not because of any misguided reliance upon astrological signs. Edgar's innate honesty and dignity make accepting Edmund's duplicity easy and prevents any questioning of Edmund's lies. Edgar cannot imagine that his brother would lie to him since Edgar would not lie to his brother. Edmund easily convinces Edgar that he should arm himself against their father, a man whom Edgar loves.

Literary Device

The double plot is an important literary device in this play. With two plots, perfectly intertwined and yet offering parallel lessons, Shakespeare is able to demonstrate the tragic consequences that result when man's law is given precedence over natural law. Eventually, Gloucester and Lear learn the importance of natural law when they recognize that they have violated these basic tenets, with both finally turning to nature to find answers for why their children have betrayed them. Their counterparts, Edmund, Goneril, Regan, and Cornwall, represent the evil that functions in violation of natural law.

The double plot serves an important function, emphasizing natural law as an essential facet of both plots. Shakespeare then uses the two plots to point to how essential an acknowledgment of natural law is in a moral society. In both plots the absence of natural law is destructive, and ultimately even those who are good cannot act to save Cordelia or the other good characters from the ravages of evil and tyranny.

Glossary

more composition the act of composing, or putting together a whole by combining parts.

speed to have good fortune; prosper; succeed.

character style of printing or handwriting.

pawn anything given as security, as for a debt, performance of an action, and so on; pledge; guaranty.

goatish lustful; lecherous.

Act I
Scene 3

Summary

Set in the palace of Goneril and the Duke of Albany, this scene opens with Goneril asking her steward, Oswald, if Lear struck him for making fun of the king's Fool. Oswald confirms the encounter. Goneril, enraged, instructs Oswald to keep Lear waiting when he needs something, and if the king is unhappy with this treatment, he should be told to move to Regan's palace. Goneril then commands her servants to treat the king's company with coldness since the knights' lewd behavior is creating a disturbance in her household.

Commentary

Goneril promises at the end of Scene 1 that if her father proves to be a nuisance, she will deal with him accordingly. In Scene 3, Goneril does just that by refusing to respond to the needs of the king and his entourage. She is calling the shots now, and Lear is never to regain control again. He may see himself as king, but Goneril views him as a doddering old fool, one she refers to as an "Idle old man" (I.3.17). Goneril treats her father with particular cruelty and callousness, not with the love and adoration she professed in order to gain control of half of his kingdom.

Character Insight

In this scene, as later in Scene 4, Goneril reveals her true character. She defies the hierarchy of nature, which calls for daughters to respect and honor their fathers, and lays the groundwork for the torment she sets in motion for the remainder of her father's life. In Goneril's defense, Lear is a poor guest. Goneril protests that his knights are riotous and that Lear complains constantly. By instructing her steward, Oswald, to make himself less accommodating, she is punishing her unruly guests. At this juncture, both father and daughter bear some fault, but Goneril has led her father to believe that her love for him extends beyond any evidence of bad behavior, and so ultimately, she is responsible for Lear's actions, having earlier endorsed them.

This scene introduces Oswald, who is clearly more familiar with Goneril than customary in a lady/steward association. Because Goneril gives Oswald the authority to treat the king rudely, it is apparent that the steward's position is not simply that of a servant. The scene opens with Goneril's reference to Oswald's chiding of the king's Fool, conduct not expected from an ordinary servant. The steward obviously runs the household, wielding a significant amount of authority over other servants. Still, Goneril expresses her desire for Oswald to act on her authority; she will answer for any problems caused by his actions.

Character Insight

Also noteworthy is the fact that Lear has been hunting, as the sounds of the hunting horns in the distance indicate. The king may be an old man, as Goneril states, but he is not infirm; nor is he idle, as she accuses him of being. Lear is obviously in good physical shape, even if not as mentally alert as he might have been in his younger years.

Glossary

idle frivolous; silly.

straight immediately.

Act I
Scene 4

Summary

The setting is a hall in Goneril's palace. Kent, earlier banished by Lear, reappears in disguise as Caius. Lear enters and begins asking Kent questions about his identity and his intent. Kent's responses are vague, but he asserts his loyalty and willingness to serve the king. Kent's obvious admiration impresses Lear.

When the king asks to see Goneril, Oswald leaves without responding to the request. A knight reports that Goneril is unwell and unavailable. The knight also tells Lear that all the members of Goneril's household are treating the king's entourage rudely.

Goneril enters, complaining about the king's Fool and his unruly knights. Goneril demands that Lear reduce the number of knights in his service. In anger, the king declares that he will pack up his people and move to Regan's palace, where he is sure to receive a warmer reception.

Commentary

In this scene, the audience sees how erratically Lear deals with problems. When Oswald ignores the king, Lear is shocked: "he would not!" (I.4.54). Lear is king, and he expects to be obeyed. Nevertheless, when he learns of the poor service afforded his knights and recalls how he, too, has been neglected by Goneril's staff, Lear says, "I will look further into't" (I.4.69). But in the next line, Lear asks, "But where's my Fool?" (I.4.69). Lear looks to the Fool to distract him with entertainment, to help him forget his problems.

Although the lack of attention and service is insulting and demeaning, the king is not prepared to confront Goneril and her steward. At other times, Lear responds to problems with outbursts of cursing, even a physical attack when provoked. The audience saw an angry Lear disown his youngest daughter in Scene 1. In this scene, Lear is almost out of control when he answers Oswald's insulting address: "My Lady's father! My lord's knave, you whoreson dog you slave, you cur!" (I.4.79–80).

Lear is helpless, at the mercy of his daughter and her servants. The once-omnipotent king has no effective means of dealing with these events, except with anger. Kings are used to making rules, not following them. And thus, Lear responds to Oswald's insults with swearing and by striking him. Another response to his dilemma is expressed in self-pity. As he finally recognizes the precariousness of his new position, Lear strikes his own head and curses his misfortune (I.4.268–270).

Lear succumbs to despair. As the play progresses, the king will lapse into other fits of self-pity and fury, and he will discover different means of dealing with the realities of the mistakes he has made. As the depth of his tragedy grows deeper, Lear will react with denial, with helplessness, with regret and apathy, and with a growing compassion for those around him.

Kent reappears, disguised in this scene. He is truly selfless, devoted to the king who earlier banished him. When queried by Lear as to his identity, Kent replies that he is "a man" (I.4.10). Thus, he is no one special, and yet, he stands apart from other men. Kent's response distinguishes him from animals, because he is not defined by desires, needs, and a willingness to simply seize whatever he wants—as animals do to survive. This characteristic sets him apart from other characters, such as Goneril, Regan, Cornwall, and Edmund, all of whom are willing to behave as beasts, taking what they want. Instead, Kent is a man defined by honesty and love for his king.

The Fool enters the play for the first time in this scene. He functions much as a Chorus would in a Greek tragedy: His role is to comment on events and the king's actions, serving in some respects as the king's conscience. The Fool requires a careful study, because he often sounds cruel as he addresses the king with sarcasm and irony. Sometimes, the Fool seems to be rubbing salt in Lear's wounds, rather than acting as the king's advocate. However, as the play progresses, the audience begins to sense how much the Fool loves the king; he will try to protect and care for Lear just as Cordelia attempts to do when she returns.

Style &
Language

The Fool's initial address to Kent makes clear that he sees Kent as the king's ally; thus he asks if Kent is in need of a fool's coxcomb (I.4.94). These lines, which focus on the coxcomb, indicate that the Fool needs a fool, and clearly Kent is one, since he seeks to follow Lear, who has neither a kingdom nor even a home. The Fool is loyal and honest, a good match for Kent, but he is also able to point out the king's faults, as no one else can. The king may threaten to have the Fool whipped (it was not unusual for the king's jester to be beaten), but the audience never regards this as a viable threat. The Fool's use of irony, sarcasm, and humor helps to ease the truth and allows him to moderate Lear's behavior as no other character can. In Scene 1, Kent's attempts to restrain Lear's actions earn banishment, but the Fool can bridle the king's unpredictable disposition more successfully.

Goneril's confrontation with her father initially invites the audience's sympathy. The king's retinue have been rude, demanding, and unappreciative guests.

Goneril accuses Lear of not only failing to control his men but also encouraging their disruptive behavior. No doubt Goneril has suffered from this misconduct, which the king refuses to address. Instead of responding to these concerns, Lear replies by asking, "Are you our daughter?" (I.4.216). The king is, after all, the king, accustomed to having his own way and behaving any way that pleases him. He does not yet acknowledge his role of guest or his diminished control under a new order. Lear doesn't grasp that a king without a kingdom has little to distinguish him from any other man. But when Goneril abruptly dismisses half his men, Lear is forced to admit that he is no longer in control.

However, any sympathy the audience might muster for Goneril dissipates when she sends Oswald to deliver a letter warning Regan of their father's pending visit. She instructs Oswald to add his own embellishments and warnings about Lear's conduct.

As the conflict between father and daughter escalates, Lear turns inward and questions who he is (I.4.223–227). Can Lear be king when he has given away his kingdom? What Lear has relied upon as truth is no longer trustworthy; his reality has changed. His daughter is not obedient, nor does she treat him with the respect due a father and a king. Even her servants deny him the high regard generally granted to a sovereign.

Style & Language

In conversation with the Fool, Lear echoes Cordelia's words from Scene 1—"Nothing, my lord" (I.1.86)—with his own—"nothing can be made of nothing" (I.4.130). Kent began this exchange with his own "nothing" (I.4.126) in response to the Fool's bit of verse. Again, "nothing" is a word with significant meaning, since already nothing has resulted in the growing tragedy. From nothing emerges the beginnings of a family tragedy, as Lear is displaced. Lear finally realizes he has treated Cordelia poorly (I.4.265) and admits his mistake.

Although he was present in Scene 1, Albany has no real role in the disbursement of the king's property. Nonetheless, the conversation in Scene 1 between Kent and Gloucester reveals that the king prefers Albany to his other son-in-law, Cornwall. In this scene, Albany attempts to calm the king, but Lear is beyond patience and refuses to listen to Albany, although he has admired him in the past. Albany obviously is concerned for the king's welfare, but he lacks the strength to stand up to his wife, Goneril, and thus, he cannot control her. Albany is Goneril's opposite, gentle and kind as compared with his wife's cruel and self-serving demeanor.

Glossary

defuse 1. complicate. 2. to render harmless.

curious highly detailed, as in workmanship; elaborate.

roundest outspoken; plain and blunt; straightforward.

bandy to give and take; specifically, to exchange (words) in an angry or argumentative manner.

coxcomb a cap topped with a notched strip of red cloth like a cock's comb, formerly worn by jesters.

besort to be suitable to.

cadent falling.

Act I
Scene 5

Summary

The setting for this brief scene is outside Goneril's palace. Lear instructs Kent to go at once to Regan's palace and deliver a letter. As Kent leaves, the Fool attempts to distract the king with silly remarks, but their content points ironically to Lear's actions. The torment of the king is obvious as he laments his treatment of Cordelia.

Lear expresses his first concerns, a premonition, for his sanity. Soon the horses are ready, and the king begins his journey to his second daughter's palace.

Commentary

In Scene 5, the king is clearly frightened and apprehensive for his future, although he continues to hope that Regan can be counted upon to provide him with sanctuary. Lear also expresses fear for his sanity: "O let me not be mad, not mad, sweet heaven! I would not be mad. Keep me in temper, I would not be mad" (I.5.43–44).

Literary Device

This appeal foreshadows events that will occur later in the play. This brief plea also contains a prayer to a divinity. Although the setting of *King Lear* predates Christianity, Lear still relies upon a god to guide and protect him. The Fool does not give Lear any respite in this scene, as he continues to remind the king of the mistakes he has made and the precarious position in which he has placed himself. The Fool appears cruel once again, but Lear finally begins to understand that his foolishness has led to this current state of affairs.

Character Insight

The king's thoughts once again turn to remorse for his behavior toward Cordelia: "I did her wrong" (I.5.24). Because this comment is offered without context, it reveals that Lear has noted a flash of insight into his own conduct, actions that he has come to regret. This brief mention of Cordelia also reminds the audience that she continues to have an important role in the play, although she will not reappear for some time.

Glossary

kibes a chapped or ulcerated chilblain especially on the heel.

Act II
Scene 1

Summary

The setting is the Earl of Gloucester's castle. As the scene opens, Curan, a courier, tells Edmund that Regan and Cornwall will be arriving that evening. Curan also mentions rumors of a feud between Cornwall and Albany.

Edmund expresses excitement over Cornwall's visit because he imagines that he can involve the duke in his plans to discredit Edgar. As a means to that end, Edmund implies brotherly concern as he coaxes Edgar to slip away under the cover of night. Edmund suggests that Cornwall suspects Edgar of aiding his enemy, Albany. Edgar, innocent and unaware of any of this plotting, agrees to flee to protect himself. In another ploy to blemish Edgar's reputation, Edmund engages his brother in a fake battle, intentionally wounding himself to draw Gloucester's sympathy.

In response to Edmund's explanation of his brother's attack, Gloucester promises to find Edgar and bring him to justice. Gloucester also pledges to make Edmund his heir.

Regan and Cornwall enter. Without hesitation, they fall for Edmund's story and join in condemning Edgar. Cornwall proclaims that Edmund shall join forces with him. Regan and Cornwall flatter Gloucester by asking his advice on an appropriate response to letters received from Lear and Goneril.

Commentary

Curan's report of strife between Albany and Cornwall helps illustrate that Lear's division of his kingdom is a mistake. Shakespeare's Elizabethan audience would have expected such a conflict since the English know, all too well, that insurrection and conflict between petty lords requires a strong centralized government to maintain control. Making

Cornwall and Albany equal, in effect co-leaders, inevitably leads to discord. Curan's disclosure is, at this moment, unimportant, except that Edmund sees the information as useful to his plotting.

Edmund, an opportunist, takes advantage of Curan's report and accelerates his plans by calling Edgar out of hiding and creating a mock battle. By self-inflicting a minor wound, Edmund makes Edgar look like a villain. Gloucester is fooled easily by the staged sounds and blood of battle. With the physical evidence before his eyes, Gloucester believes Edmund's story.

Edmund also convinces his father of Edgar's attack by carefully selecting his words:

Style & Language

> Spoke with how manifold and strong a bond
> The child was bound to th' father; Sir in fine,
> Seeing how loathly opposite I stood
> To his unnatural purpose, in fell motion,
> With his prepared sword he charges home
> My unprovided body, launch'd arm. (II.1.46–51)

Theme

Here, Edmund speaks as a hero, the so-called "good guy," who stands up to evil at the risk of his own life. In Shakespeare's time, the testimony of a legitimate son would weigh more significantly than that of an illegitimate son; but in this instance, Edgar is not available to present his position. Gloucester easily accepts the illegitimate son's words, while rejecting a lifetime of evidence of Edgar's worthiness, illustrating how out of step the world has become with nature. According to natural order, years of devotion and love should lead to trust, but with the events of Act I, fathers no longer trust their children's love. Instead, fathers are easily fooled into rejecting the children who love them most. Lear has rejected the daughter who genuinely loves him, and now, Gloucester has rejected the son who genuinely loves him. These events further support the idea that Lear's earlier actions have rejected the natural order of the world.

Regan and Cornwall's visit gives Edmund another opportunity to advance his plot. In this scene, Regan and Cornwall appear to be conscientious and reasonable people. Regan seems genuinely upset to learn of Edgar's betrayal. That Regan has come seeking Gloucester's advice also adds to her credibility because it creates the impression that she values the older man's guidance.

Cornwall's acceptance of Edmund's story and his welcoming of Edmund into his clique foreshadow the evil that will emerge from Cornwall and provide a hint to the audience that Cornwall is not the nice guy he appears to be. As for Edmund, Cornwall's invitation offers him the chance to ally himself with Cornwall. Since Albany attempted to intercede on the king's behalf in Act I, the audience expects Cornwall to emerge as a villain, and his alliance with Edmund emphasizes that both men are evil figures. Gloucester, playing the part of a gullible old man, has no real reason to distrust either Edmund or Cornwall—neither has proven untrustworthy in the past.

Glossary

briefness sudden action; a short duration or length.

bend 1. to turn or direct. 2. to cause to have a fixed purpose; determine; aim.

faith'd approved; endorsed.

il affected unfaithful.

Act II
Scene 2

Summary

The setting is just outside Gloucester's castle. Kent and Oswald arrive separately to deliver letters to Regan. Oswald does not immediately recognize Kent. The steward is confused when Kent denounces him and condemns his lack of integrity. When Oswald denies knowing him, Kent draws his sword and begins to beat the steward.

Oswald's cries for help draw the attention of the castle's occupants, who come to his rescue. In answer to Cornwall's query about the encounter, Kent attacks Oswald's personality, his lack of honesty, and even his appearance. Cornwall defends Oswald and orders that Kent be placed in stocks. Gloucester intervenes, reminding Regan and Cornwall that the king will consider their action against his messenger as an indignity, but Regan suggests that insulting Goneril's steward is a more grievous offense. All exit but Gloucester, who apologizes to Kent for his mistreatment. When he is left alone, Kent reads a letter from Cordelia, which promises that she will somehow intervene on her father's behalf.

Commentary

Initially, Oswald appears to be the wronged party, while Kent is a rude thug, just looking to start a fight. This misconception illustrates the purpose of Kent's presence in Act I, where the audience is permitted to view the real Kent, honest and loyal. In both the play's opening scene and later, in his defense of Cordelia, Kent defines himself with integrity; thus, the audience recognizes that Kent's abusive behavior has a meaning beyond the obvious. In reality, Kent is a loyal lord to his king, but in this instance, it is important that he remain in disguise. However, Kent knows that Oswald is carrying letters that will be used against the king, and whether in disguise or not, Kent will not lie. Thus, Kent's attack on Oswald is a reaction to the steward's dishonesty and to his purpose in fulfilling Goneril's orders. Oswald's character is evil, and Kent's reaction, while seemingly unwarranted, is in keeping with his own highly developed sense of morality.

Character Insight

Oswald, on the other hand, is Goneril's toady, and he is willingly rude to the king. Accordingly, the audience knows that, while appearing pleasant enough, the steward is a henchman without honor. Oswald adds to this negative perception when he fails to defend himself against Kent's attack. When his cries for help attract Cornwall, Oswald then lies that he has spared his attacker's life because Kent is an old man. All of these events portray Oswald as weak and dishonest. Oswald is, as Kent suggests, a parasite who thrives off Goneril's evil machinations and who makes her deceit easier to maintain.

The confrontation between Kent and Cornwall gives the audience a clearer idea of Cornwall's true character. Cornwall's mistrust of Kent's honest speech assumes that, by saying what he means, Kent must be lying. This response to Kent's plain and truthful declarations indicates that Cornwall, who uses artifice as a substitute for honesty in his own speech, cannot recognize truth when he hears it. Cornwall assumes that, because he is willing to lie and often does so, that all other men must do the same.

Placing Kent in the stocks is a serious affront to the king, akin to administering the same punishment to the king himself. This blatant act of treason perfectly illustrates how Lear's control over his subjects is crumbling. Traditionally, the king's emissary is the king *in loco*, and is accorded every respect and honor given the king, were he present. So, Kent must be treated as the king, since when the king is not present, his emissary represents him and deserves the same treatment that Lear would receive. Placing Kent in the stocks is the same as placing Lear in the stocks. This action is a serious insult to the king.

Theme

In this instance, Kent's public humiliation also demeans and insults the king. The imprisonment is an offense against nature, because the king should be accorded the respect of his subjects, just as the father is to be accorded the respect of his children, and just as the aged should be afforded the respect of the younger members of society. Cornwall's actions reflect the upheaval occurring in nature, where the old are no longer revered and the king is no longer honored. Lear is, indeed, in grave danger from Cornwall.

The scene ends with Kent reading a letter from Cordelia, but how Cordelia has learned of Lear's difficulty in this short span of time is not evident. The audience is expected to simply accept the incongruity of the letter's existence.

Glossary

finical finicky.

cullionly low, contemptible.

carbonado to cut gashes in; slash; hack.

flesh to begin; activate.

jakes an outdoor toilet; privy.

silly-ducking submissive.

Act II
Scene 3

Summary

The scene opens on Edgar, alone in the woods. In his soliloquy, Edgar relates that he is aware of his outlaw status. Thus far, he has escaped capture by hiding in the "happy hollow of a tree" (II.3.2), but he knows that to remain free, he must mask himself.

Edgar lays forth a plan in which he will disguise himself as a Bedlam beggar, smearing dirt on his face and body, tying his hair in knots, and covering his body with a blanket. In this costume, he will be known as Poor Tom.

Commentary

With Gloucester and Cornwall's men pursuing him, Edgar hides in the hollow of a tree. Believing that no one will look closely at a deranged beggar, Edgar covers himself with dirt, signs of injury, and a blanket as his humble attire. During Shakespeare's time, lunatics were assumed to be possessed by evil spirits and unable to feel pain, hence the self-mutilation as part of Edgar's disguise.

The choice to assume a mantle of madness provides Edgar with the perfect disguise, but the decision also parallels the loss of sanity that soon envelops Lear. The difference will be one of choice and invention: Lear will not be pretending. As Edgar clothes himself in madness, he becomes Poor Tom and ceases to be Edgar. The change is essential if Edgar is to move safely out of hiding while investigating the wrongful accusations against him. As Poor Tom, Edgar has a chance at survival. As Edgar, he is doomed.

Edgar ends his soliloquy with "That's something yet: Edgar I nothing am" (II.3.21). To survive under his new circumstances, Edgar must cease to exist. He quite literally becomes "nothing" in becoming Poor Tom. His previous life ceases to exist, to be nothing, and, as Tom, he is also nothing, since those who are mad exist in a world in which nothing is as it seems.

Glossary

pricks any of various pointed objects, as a thorn, goad, and so on.

bans curses.

Act II
Scene 4

Summary

Lear and his followers arrive at Gloucester's castle. Kent hails the king, who promptly asks who has placed his messenger in stocks. Lear refuses to believe that Regan and Cornwall would imprison and humiliate someone in the king's employ.

Regan and Cornwall decline speaking to the king, claiming fatigue from their journey. While Gloucester searches out the couple and secures Kent's release, the king's Fool presents a steady commentary on surrounding events—in prose and verse.

Ushered to the scene by Gloucester, Regan greets her father with seeming affection, and Lear details the sorrow that Goneril has caused him. Regan urges Lear to restrain himself and behave as befits a man of his age. Regan also advises Lear to seek Goneril's forgiveness, which provokes the king to anger and cursing. With Oswald and Goneril now present, Cornwall admits to Lear that he ordered Kent's punishment.

Lear's disgust and disillusionment are further compounded when Regan refuses to host her father and his full complement of knights. Goneril, conspiring with her sister, proposes that Lear dismiss his entire entourage. The king, angered by his daughters' rejection, calls for his horse. Lear states that he would rather live outside under the stars or beg shelter in France than stay in the company of those who disrespect his proper place as father and king. Regan and Goneril instruct Gloucester not to stop their father from venturing into the night. Regan and Goneril remain unmoved and unconcerned that the old king is going forth into a severe storm.

Commentary

As in Act I, Scene 4, the audience is permitted to observe Lear's intense, unstable reactions to adversity. He is initially bewildered by Regan and Cornwall's absence, since Lear sent advance notice of his arrival. This departure from accepted rules of hospitality truly upsets the king. Next, Lear is amazed to discover that Cornwall is responsible for placing Kent in the stocks. At several points, Lear is so angry he can hardly speak (II.4.92–93, 100–101) and he can barely compose a rational sentence. The suggestion that he return to Goneril's palace infuriates Lear. He is most impassioned when he urges divine retribution against Goneril (II.4.159–160, 162–165). Although Lear had earlier made some small effort to regain control (II.4.55–56), he cannot maintain composure in Goneril's presence.

In many respects, Lear is in denial, as when he seeks an excuse for Cornwall's behavior: "may be he is not well" (II.4.102). And when Goneril appears, Lear first pleads with her for sympathy, and then indulges in self-pity: "Art not asham'd to look upon this beard?" (II.4.188–191). Even more pleading and self-pity is evident in his later address to both daughters: "You see here, you Gods, a poor old man, / As full of grief as age; wretched in both!" (II.4.270–271).

Anger has not moved either Regan or Goneril, and groveling will be similarly ineffective, but Lear desperately tries to regain some order in a life in which he has abdicated control. In many ways, Lear appears almost resigned, as he acknowledges that Goneril is "my flesh, my blood, my daughter" (II.4.219). But he also concedes that she is of "my corrupted blood" (II.4.223), and thus, he accepts responsibility for her actions. His choices as her father have determined her choices as his daughter. All of these emotional responses cannot change the reality of his new life, nor do they provide an effective way to deal with solving the problems created by his hasty actions in Act I.

Lear tries to retain the rights and demeanor of a king, although he remains king in name only. When he orders that Regan and Cornwall appear, he expects them to do so. But Gloucester's response—"I have inform'd them so" (II.4.95)—indicates a new order. Regan agrees to speak to the king, but clearly on her terms. Lear wants to remain in charge of his destiny, even though the choices he makes are poor or filled with danger.

Lear ventures out into the storm of his own accord, although Cornwall makes certain that any prospect of return for sanctuary is met with locked doors. The king would rather face a dark and turbulent night, even if it means sleeping in the open, than keep the company of daughters who require that he give up his followers.

Character Insight

Regan initially appears to be a more sympathetic and gentle daughter. She greets Lear with politeness, but her deportment is deceptive. Regan has no real reverence for her royal father. Goneril has already revealed herself to be openly harsh and unyielding, but Regan is more competent at deception, easily assuming the mantle of respect and politeness that a gracious daughter is expected to display. And yet, the results are still the same. Her kindness is only a momentary deception. Like Goneril, Regan proves herself to be unyielding and cruel. Neither shows any love, tenderness, understanding, or gratitude toward their father who gave them his entire kingdom.

In this section, Shakespeare focuses on what loyalty means to several of these characters. Gloucester is depicted as an impotent old man, given to making peace and offering soothing remarks. He is loyal to Lear, but ineffectual in his loyalty. Kent is also loyal to the king and rejects the Fool's advice to find a protector who is on the ascent and not the descent. It is possible to regard the Fool's advice as a test of Kent's loyalty. If this is a test, Kent easily passes. Kent is loyal to the king, as is the Fool, who declines to take his own advice—because he is a fool, he says. In fact, the suggestion that Kent should find a protector who is on the ascent is what Edmund has already done. Edmund sees Cornwall as the stronger of the sisters' husbands, and so he links his prospects to those of Cornwall. But, unlike Gloucester, Kent, and the Fool, Edmund's ultimate loyalty is to himself.

Literary Device

The coming storm signals the disarray in Lear's life. He is a sad character, unable to slow the momentum of the events he has set in motion. Lear sets out into the storm in an effort to regain some purpose in his life before it slips away. Lear's bewilderment at his circumstance, the loss of his daughter's respect, and the loss of his kingship all serve to make Lear a sympathetic character. His attempts to retain dignity, rather than dismiss his knights—which represent the kingliness and power of his previous life—add to this sense of sympathy. He leaves into the storm, and rather than wait for his daughters to reject him one more time, he rejects them. In leaving, Lear attempts to seize some small control over his life. The storm is the perfect venue for Lear. Nature, which has established the natural order for king and father, has also made man a creature dependent on love for survival. The king's daughters, who are unnatural in their lack of allegiance to their father and who have rejected the bonds of blood or social order, have deprived Lear of the love and respect that he feels he deserves and that he expects. In his moment of despair, Lear turns to nature for escape.

Glossary

nether-stocks tights or stockings.

meiny attendants, collectively; retinue or household.

fetches tricks; dodges.

remotion 1. the act of removing. 2. inaccessibility.

offices the function or characteristic action of a particular thing.

Act III
Scene 1

Summary

The setting is the heath in a raging storm. Conversing with a gentleman—a character conveniently placed to enlighten Kent and the audience—Kent learns that Lear and his Fool are out in the storm. Kent relates that Albany and Cornwall are pretending amicability. Kent also divulges that the king of France has been apprised of this information and is moving with an invasion force to offer assistance to Lear. Kent instructs the gentleman to go quickly to Dover, and when there, to make known the treatment that Lear has suffered. Kent gives the messenger a ring for delivery to Cordelia. This signet jewelry will disclose Kent's identity. Kent leaves to search for Lear.

Commentary

Literary
Device

The previous scene opened with the lines "Who's there, besides foul weather?" (III.1.1), and now in this scene, we are presented with an image of Lear on the heath, his despair and rage clearly equaling the fury of the storm. The king's appearance, reflecting the turmoil of a familial tragedy, is as ravaged as the natural landscape under the assault of the storm. It is clear from the description that the storm is fierce, but so too is Lear's grief. However, Lear is not alone, and so, we also learn that the Fool shares his master's fate, to be cast out into the storm. In the Fool's earlier appearances, he functioned much as a Greek Chorus would, commenting upon the action and pointing out to Lear when he has erred. But in this scene, there is a new reason for the Fool's existence. As he attempts to ease his king's plight, it becomes clear that the Fool's new purpose is to protect Lear until Cordelia can arrive to help her father.

This scene answers the lingering question from Act II Scene 2: How does Cordelia learn so quickly of her father's tragedy? Kent tells the gentleman that spies have been sent from France to observe the treatment of the king. Kent's story is somewhat vague and suggests an improbable timeframe because word of the past few days' events could not have traveled to France so rapidly. However, Shakespeare often manipulates time in his tragedies to move the play along purposely. In this case, the expectation of an invasion and the prospect of Cordelia's arrival provide hope that Lear's situation will soon improve.

Kent also mentions a possible crack in the alliance between Albany and Cornwall, although they have sought to keep the information private. The audience has heard hints that Albany might not be as ruthless as Cornwall, but at this time, we have no reason to believe that Albany would spare Lear. If the two dukes are trying to conceal a possible rift, they may be working closely together—making Albany equally untrustworthy.

Glossary

snuffs disputes; squabbles.

bemadding maddening.

plain to complain.

out wall outside; exterior.

Act III
Scene 2

Summary

The storm continues on the heath. Lear's mood matches the intensity of nature's turbulence as he rages against his daughters' abusive treatment. The Fool attempts to reason with his king, noting that the shelter of a dry house, even one gained by losing face, is superior to a stay in the storm's fury. But Lear will have no part of submission, especially before his daughters. Kent arrives and points to a nearby hovel, which promises some protection, while he returns to Gloucester's castle to ask that they admit the king. The Fool, alone, remains on stage to proclaim a prophecy.

Commentary

Once again, the audience observes how Lear copes with the swell of problems besieging him. The scene opens on Lear in the midst of wind, rain, and personal despair. As he calls upon the storm to unleash its fury on the world, he also cries out for the destruction of ungrateful man: "Crack nature's moulds, all germens spill at once / That make ingrateful man!" (III.2.8–9). By destroying the molds that nature uses to create men, the genetic code of life will be lost. In this instance, Lear is without hope; his despondency is so great that it approaches nihilism, a belief in nothing.

Lear continues to wallow in self-pity as he labels himself "A poor, infirm, weak, and despis'd old man" (III.2.20). Lear willingly submits to the strength of the storm rather than seek shelter or fight for his sanity. He has fallen so far from the strong monarch who began the play that he has strength only to wish for utter destruction. And yet, Lear remains a sympathetic character, one who fears for his own mental balance—"My wits begin to turn" (III.2.68)—and one also who can express concern for his companion's comfort—"How dost my boy? Art cold?" (III.2.68).

In spite of his pitiful state, Lear is revealed as a complex man, one whose punishment far exceeds his foolish errors, and thus, Lear is deserving of the audience's sympathy. The Fool's final speech presents a contrast between the reality of the world he and Lear are experiencing and a utopian world, where justice and goodness replace evil.

Glossary

cataracts floodgate (of heaven).

vaunt-couriers a forerunner; precursor.

fire extreme suffering or distress that tries one's endurance; tribulation or ordeal.

punder confusion; excitement.

Act III
Scene 3

Summary

The setting is Gloucester's castle, where Gloucester and Edmund are conversing. Gloucester tells his son that when he asked Regan and Cornwall to leave, so that he might offer aid to Lear, they seized his house. Now Gloucester is little more than a prisoner in his own home, forbidden to even speak to the king. Gloucester also tells Edmund that he has heard of a plan to revenge the king's injuries, unaware that he is divulging the plans to a traitor. Gloucester exits. Alone, Edmund plans to gain Cornwall's favor by revealing the plan to aid the king.

Commentary

Character Insight

At the beginning of the play, Gloucester appears weak and foolish, easily fooled by Edmund. In Act I, his boasts about easy conquests misleads the audience into dismissing Gloucester as a silly old man; but in this scene, the earl seems worthy of the king's allegiance. Gloucester proves that he is willing to sacrifice his own life for the king by disobeying Regan and Cornwall. This genuinely heroic behavior sets Gloucester apart from Edmund. An opportunist, Edmund takes advantage of his father's trust, seizing the chance to win Cornwall's favor. Betraying his father will provide Edmund with the position and wealth he craves. Acting without hesitation, Edmund sets out on a course that belies his breeding; a triumph of conscience is not a likely prospect in his unfolding treachery.

Glossary

footed secured.

Act III
Scene 4

Summary

Although Kent directs Lear to a hovel for shelter, the king refuses to protect himself from the storm.

The Fool runs from the hovel, exclaiming that a spirit has taken possession of the shelter. The spirit, who soon emerges, is Edgar disguised as Poor Tom, pitiful pauper. The king tears off his own clothing, making himself look more like the unclad Poor Tom.

Gloucester enters the scene, carrying a torch. He has found both warm shelter and food for the king, but Lear declines, claiming that he needs to talk more with the Bedlam beggar. The disguised Edgar complains of the cold and everyone moves into the shelter.

Commentary

Much of this scene focuses on Lear's mental disintegration. Once again, Lear deals with his personal tragedy in a variety of ways. For the first time, Lear focuses his attention on others' lives, those who are as wretched as the king himself:

> Poor naked wretches, wherso'er you are,
> That bide the pelting of this pitiless storm,
> How shall your houseless heads and unfed sides,
> Your loo'd and window'd raggedness, defend you
> From seasons such as these? (III.4.28–32)

Style & Language

These words are regretful, remorseful, empathetic, and compassionate for the poor, a population that Lear has not noticed before. Lear recognizes the parallels between their lives and his current situation. In a real sense, his pity for the poor is also a reflection of the pity he feels for his own situation. He finally feels compassion for the poor, only because he has become one of them.

With this extension of pity comes a new social awareness. Lear realizes that he has done nothing to aid the poor people in his kingdom. Instead, he has contributed their demise. He chastises himself saying:

O! I have ta'en
Too little care of this. Take physic, Pomp;
Expose thyself to feel what wretches feel,
That thou mayst shake the superflux to them,
And show the heavens more just. (III.4.32–36)

Character Insight

Lear acknowledges that justice comes from man and heaven. Lear is the anointed king, God's representative, and thus, shares the responsibility for dispensing justice on earth. He recognizes that he bears responsibility for both his own problems and for those of others, who suffer equally. Once again, Lear is revealed as a complex and sympathetic figure, one who defies easy definition.

With his new knowledge, Lear would be a more effective king. But because he has given up his royal position, he can take responsibility only for his present situation. His inability to right the wrongs he has inflicted upon his people contributes to his fall into madness. The turmoil in Lear's mind makes him oblivious to the weather storm that surrounds him, and his waning lucidity also provides an escape from the reality of his plight.

Literary Device

When Poor Tom emerges from the hovel, Lear sees a mirror image of himself. Lear identifies with Poor Tom because both men have lost everything. Lear imagines that Tom is also the victim of deceitful and cruel daughters. Lear's identity with Tom is absolute when he removes his clothing to join Tom in near-nakedness. This inability to distinguish himself from Tom is a symptom of Lear's madness. This scene reminds the audience that very little separates man from beast. The fragility of man is inescapable, because only a fine line divides civilized and uncivilized states.

Character Insight

Although parallels can be drawn between Gloucester's situation and Lear's circumstances (as both men are being manipulated by their children), one notable difference remains: Gloucester retains his sanity. Gloucester is aware of how easily he might lose his mind, and he fears it may happen yet (III.4.62–63), but he has an inner strength that Lear does not have, which permits him to survive.

Paradoxically, Gloucester fails to recognize his own son, Edgar, disguised as Poor Tom. This scene builds upon Scene 3 by showing Gloucester's determination to help the old king, but it also reveals a father in as much pain as the king. Gloucester is not aware that his own situation will turn disastrous soon.

Glossary

taking contagious; infectious.

out-paramour'd having more lovers or mistresses.

plackets pockets, especially in a woman's skirt or a petticoat.

lendings things that one has let another have use of temporarily and on condition that they, or equivalents, be returned.

first cock midnight.

green mantle a surface covered with scum or froth.

Act III
Scene 5

Summary

The setting is Gloucester's castle. Edmund betrays his father and wins Cornwall's approval by releasing the details of France's plan to aid the king. As reward, Edmund gains Gloucester's title and lands.

Commentary

In this scene, both Edmund and Cornwall pretend to be virtuous, as each attempts to justify his disloyalty. Clearly, Gloucester and Lear are both victims of two self-serving men—Edmund and Cornwall. Edmund, feigning regret for having betrayed his father, laments that his nature, which is to honor his father, must now be subordinate to the loyalty he feels for his country. Thus, Edmund makes excuses for betraying his own father. Cornwall's presence serves to reinforce Edmund's choice, when he suggests that perhaps Edgar is justified to seek his father's murder. Cornwall sees Gloucester's actions as treasonous, and describes him as having a "reproveable badness" (III.5.6). This pronouncement from Cornwall endorses Edmund's treachery toward his father, and also provides Edmund with a sort of self-righteous justice.

Glossary

apprehension capture or arrest.

blood parental heritage; family line; lineage.

Act III
Scene 6

Summary

Gloucester sets out to find food, leaving the king and his party in a farmhouse next to the castle.

The Fool and Edgar take part in Lear's mock trial of Regan and Goneril. Gloucester enters and reveals that he has learned of a plot to kill the king. The group prepares to take Lear to Dover, where friends can come to his aid.

Commentary

Edmund's gibberish about foul fiends certainly fits both Edgar and Lear's circumstances, since both have been victims of deceit and wickedness. Once they all come in out of the storm, Lear abandons his plans for seeking physical revenge, and instead, decides to place Goneril and Regan on trial. The audience might consider a mock trial as further evidence of Lear's madness; but a trial is typically a search for the truth—and, often, a search for the motive or reason for an action. Lear, like so many victims, needs to know why this tragedy has happened. Did he deserve such abuse from his daughters? Did his actions contribute in some way to their evil attitudes? To Lear, gaining a grasp of the truth may lead the way to restoring his sanity.

Lear appoints the disguised Edgar and the Fool as judges, and begins the trial of Goneril, whom Lear accuses of kicking him. But the blow Goneril gave to her father was not physical; her injury was to his heart and soul. Lear urges the judges to "anatomize Regan, to see what breeds about her heart" (III.6.74–75). Lear's words are pointed and painful. Edgar cannot continue to participate, and even the Fool falls silent. Finally, Lear is so exhausted by the strain of the mock trial that he decides to pause for a much-needed rest.

Character Insight

This is the last appearance of the Fool. In his final line, he predicts his death: "I'll go to bed at noon" (III.6.83). The play never reveals whether the Fool actually dies, since the lines in Act V Scene 3—"And my poor fool is hang'd" (V.3.304)—refer to Cordelia's death. The Fool has fulfilled his role, stepping in to take Cordelia's place after her banishment and disappearing as she reappears. Both Cordelia and the Fool are caretakers for Lear, and when one is present, the other need not be.

Literary Device

Lear and his allies heed Gloucester's warning that the king must flee to Dover. With the king and his forces gone, Gloucester is left alone to face Cornwall's wrath. After Gloucester also exits, Edgar is left alone on stage. His soliloquy ties together the two parallel plots and points to the similarities between his situation and that of the king's: "He childed as I father'd!" (III.6.108). The king has cruel children, while Edgar has a cruel father, but Edgar realizes his situation is insignificant compared with that of the king, who has lost both his rule and his mind.

Glossary

yokefellow a companion, partner, or associate.

minikin very small and delicate; diminutive.

joint-stool a stool made with jointed parts.

trundle-tail a dog with a curled tail.

portable bearable; endurable.

Act III
Scene 7

Summary

The setting moves back to Gloucester's castle. Cornwall is dispatching Goneril with a letter to Albany, telling him of the invasion by the King of France. Cornwall orders that Gloucester be found and brought to him.

Edmund is told to accompany Goneril so that he is not present for Gloucester's punishment. Before Edmund and Goneril can leave, Oswald enters with news that Gloucester has warned the king and aided his escape to Dover.

As soon as Gloucester appears on the scene, Cornwall orders him bound to a chair. Regan viciously plucks at Gloucester's beard, calling him a traitor.

Intensifying the torture, Cornwall gouges out one of Gloucester's eyes. When a servant tries to stop the torment, Regan draws a sword and murders the steward. Cornwall gouges out Gloucester's other eye.

When the old man calls out to Edmund for help, Regan reveals that it was Edmund who betrayed his father. At this, Gloucester finally understands that he has misjudged Edgar. After throwing Gloucester out to find his own way to Dover, Regan helps Cornwall, who was wounded in the fray, and both leave for Dover.

Commentary

The full impact of this scene cannot be felt in a reading of the play text. The brutality of Gloucester's blinding must be seen and heard on stage for the audience to fully appreciate the evil being manifested by Cornwall and Regan. Both Goneril and Regan are especially cruel and bloodthirsty, as they call for Gloucester's punishment: "Hang him instantly. [Regan] / Pluck out his eyes [Goneril]" (III.7.4–5).

Having heard these two vultures call out for his father's blood, Edmund must have understood how harsh a punishment Gloucester is about to endure. And yet, Edmund willingly and easily leaves on his errand. This scene illustrates Edmund's wickedness; he must appreciate the true measure of Cornwall's evil and his father's vulnerability in the face of Cornwall's anger.

Cornwall's villainy in this scene is not unexpected. His anger earlier in Act III builds to the brink of losing control; in this scene, the audience sees Regan's husband refusing any attempts at civility. He has become the beast that is lurking just beneath the veneer of civilization. Cornwall appears to recognize that he lacks the authority to put Gloucester to death:

> Though well we may not pass upon his life
> Without the form of justice, yet our power
> Shall do a court'sy to our wrath, which men
> May blame but not control. (III.7.24–27)

Character Insight

Still, Cornwall argues that he is provoked and must gratify his wrath. When Gloucester is brought to him, Cornwall makes no attempt to control himself. Although Gloucester reminds Cornwall that they are guests in his home, neither Cornwall nor Regan has any interest in maintaining the rules of hospitality. Regan's plucking of Gloucester's beard reinforces the point that she has no basic respect for age or rank. Gloucester is an earl and an elderly statesman, and Regan's pulling of his beard further rejects the structure of nature, which provides that the older members of a society be revered for their age and wisdom. Gloucester recognizes the insult saying, "'tis most ignobly done" (III.7.35).

Gloucester has faith in divine justice, just as Lear has implored the gods for justice. Nonetheless, justice appears to be lacking at several points throughout *King Lear*, and the plucking of Gloucester's eyes is certainly one instance. Gloucester has made many errors in judgment, but in this case, as with Lear, the punishment is surely in excess of his mistakes. When Regan reveals Edmund's treason, Gloucester is quick to recognize his folly, much quicker than Lear.

Literary Device

The plucking out of Gloucester's eyes is so brutal that not even Cornwall's servants can stand by without acting. Regan, Goneril, and Cornwall's brutal natures have been evident all along, with each act of wickedness building upon the previous. And so, the audience is not totally unprepared for these events. But in spite of the hints, no one can be ready for Cornwall ripping out Gloucester's eyes and stomping them under his boot. This is a scene of particular brutality, matched only by the bloodthirsty brutality of certain scenes in Shakespeare's Latin plays, especially *Titus Andronicus*.

Interestingly, Regan shows some real humanity, though briefly, when Cornwall is wounded. Her solicitous question—"How is't my Lord. How look you?" (III.7.92)—reveals that she is not totally self-serving or incapable of love and compassion—virtually the only instance where Regan appears human.

Glossary

festinate hurried.

questrists seekers; pursuers.

ruffle to disturb, irritate, or annoy; to take away the smoothness of; wrinkle; ripple.

dearn gloomy; bleak.

Act IV
Scene 1

Summary

The setting is the heath. A blinded Gloucester is led by an elderly man, one of his tenants. The ailing earl laments that he treated Edgar badly and wishes for the opportunity to once again touch his son, since he can no longer see him. Gloucester hears Edgar's voice and remembers Poor Tom from the night of the storm. In an act of humanity, Gloucester sends his tenant for some clothing so that the Bedlam beggar might be covered.

Gloucester is concerned that the Old Man might suffer for having given assistance, so he dismisses him and asks Tom to be his guide to Dover, where he seeks the highest cliff. Tom agrees to take Gloucester to the cliff.

Commentary

Literary Device

Edgar's opening soliloquy reveals his belief that having survived the worst that fortune can throw at him, nothing more terrible can happen; but in fact, Edgar's acceptance of fortune is tested when the blinded Gloucester is led in. When he sees his father's condition, Edgar is forced to admit that his situation has disintegrated even further. Gloucester is being led by a tenant, who refuses to leave although his own life is at risk. Their conversation supplies a paradox:

You cannot see your way. [Old Man]

I have no way, and therefore want no eyes; [Gloucester]

I stumbled when I saw. (IV.1.17–19)

Character Insight

These lines illustrate Gloucester's failing. When he had his vision, he could not see the deceit fabricated by his younger son, and thus, vision has not helped him see his way in the past. Now that he has lost his vision but finally seen the truth, Gloucester can envision no way in which he can regain the elder son, who is lost to him. For Gloucester, the disadvantage of lost sight has become an advantage (IV.1.20–21), and his only wish is that he might "live to see thee [Edgar] in my touch" (IV.1.23).

In many ways, Gloucester's response to his tragedy parallels Lear's. Like Lear, Gloucester feels despair and questions gods who can "kill us for their sport" (IV.1.37). And like Lear, Gloucester finds his humanity in the midst of his tragedy. The blinded old man who asks that clothing be brought, so that Poor Tom might be covered, is a very different man from the Gloucester of Act I. In the play's opening scene, the earl boasted about the good sport to be had at Edmund's illegitimate conception. Instead of a thoughtless braggart, Gloucester is filled with compassion for Poor Tom (IV.1.63–70).

This compassion for his fellow man indicates that Gloucester regrets the behavior of his past, as he seeks to make amends by sharing with those he never noticed before. This action parallels the self-awareness that moved Lear to suddenly consider the poor and disadvantaged in Act III, Scene 4. Like Lear, Gloucester questions divine justice, feels despair, evokes nihilism (the belief that life is without reason or purpose), and discovers his own humanity. This scene demonstrates dramatically the parallelism between the primary plot and the subplot.

Glossary

daub it further disguise it further.

horse-way horse path.

superfluous extravagant; prodigal.

bending overhanging; prominent.

Act IV
Scene 2

Summary

The setting is just outside the Duke of Albany's palace, where Goneril and Edmund are now present. Oswald enters with news that Albany is a changed man. The steward relates that Albany was pleased to learn of the proposed invasion by France and displeased when he learned that Gloucester had been replaced by his younger son Edmund, who had betrayed his father. With this announcement, Goneril takes command of her forces and orders Edmund to return to Cornwall while she deals with Albany. As they part, Goneril gives Edmund a favor of her affection and a farewell kiss. After Edmund leaves, Goneril remarks on the favorable impression he makes compared with her weakling husband.

Albany enters and angrily accuses Goneril of being an unnatural daughter. He also accuses Goneril and Regan of being like tigers, who have attacked their aged father. A messenger enters with the announcement that Cornwall has died of the wounds he suffered after blinding Gloucester. Albany is aghast at the news of Gloucester's torture and calls Cornwall's death divine justice. Albany vows revenge against Edmund for leaving Gloucester at the mercy of Cornwall.

Commentary

Goneril is attracted to the young, handsome, and obedient Edmund. Such qualities make him more attractive to her than her own husband. Goneril expects obedience from a man, but she also wants strength and a willingness to take what he desires—characteristics that match her own. The fact that Goneril is married does not appear to be a concern. The steward's news that Albany's political and personal alliances have changed only make Edmund more appealing to Goneril.

Albany's initial remarks to Goneril reveal how much he has changed from the beginning of the play. Albany's previous hesitation to confront his wife is now replaced by direct address of her wickedness: "You are not worth the dust which the rude wind / blows in your face." (IV.2.31-32). His attack on Goneril's integrity shows that Albany is a highly moral and humane individual, the antithesis of his wife, and an individual the audience has not witnessed earlier in the play. In his attack on Goneril, Albany's view of nature is the opposite of his wife's. Where Goneril has created chaos, Albany endorses nature's design and a view of nature's work within an organic framework:

> That nature, which contemns it origin,
> Cannot be border'd certain in itself;
> She that herself will sliver and disbranch
> From her material sap, perforce must wither
> And come to deadly use. (IV.2.32–36)

Albany accepts that nature's pattern is essential for survival. The hierarchy of father to child, king to subject, God to king, is essential to eliminating chaos of the world. Goneril has reversed that natural order in her treatment of Lear, and the resulting chaos and anarchy has turned man against himself.

Albany points out that the news that Cornwall is dead is evidence of divine justice, and this event should provide a warning to Goneril, but she ignores Albany's words to focus on the greater concern—Regan as a widow is now available to marry Edmund. Goneril on the other hand, does have a husband, one whom she expects to control. Goneril is heir to one-half the kingdom, and she expects Albany to remember that this was her dowry; but he is stronger than Cornwall. And although Albany hesitated earlier to confront Goneril when he thought she was wrong, he is not the willing participant in evil that Cornwall has shown himself to be. Albany is genuinely shocked when he learns of Gloucester's blinding, while Cornwall easily succumbed to this perversion.

With this new resistance to his wife, Albany joins the ranks of characters who have undergone dramatic change during the course of the play, growing and evolving into a stronger and more compassionate individual. As the highest-ranking nobleman remaining, Albany will have no choice but to defend England against the French invasion. But this scene signals that Albany's loyalties will not be with his wife but with those who defend Lear.

Goneril's role, here, is in contrast to that of most Elizabethan women. In this period, women were totally subordinate to their husband's desires. The chain of authority was from God to king, king to subject (always male) and male to women and children. Elizabeth I refused to marry rather than be subject to any man's authority. Goneril, however, sees herself as the ultimate authority, and this contradicts the reality of this historical period.

Glossary

cowish timid; cowardly.

answer any act in response or retaliation.

sliver to cut or break into slivers.

bending to turn or direct.

justicers legal officials; judges.

Act IV
Scene 3

Summary

The setting is the French camp near Dover. Kent hears that the king of France has been forced to return to his own country. Kent asks a Gentleman if, upon reading his letters, Cordelia revealed any emotion, and learns that she did manage to keep her feelings under control. Kent responds by acknowledging the stars' influence, which have made Cordelia so different from her sisters. Kent, who is still disguised, states that he will bring the Gentleman to Lear in Dover, and at the proper time, he will reveal his own identity.

Commentary

The King of France must return to his own country because a French invasion of England would be far too offensive for an audience still sensitive about a Spanish intrusion in recent years. The reason for the king's return is unimportant, and hence the vagueness in this scene's opening lines. The critical point is that Cordelia could not have her husband present to cloud the reunion with her father or to intrude on the final scene of the play. While the Marshal of France has been left to command the forces, the point is understood that Cordelia, who is English, will lead the defense of her father.

At Kent's request, the Gentleman reveals Cordelia's response to news of her father's treatment. Her tears and pensive retreat prove her compassion and establish that she is, indeed, the opposite of her sisters. Kent takes the difference one step further by pointing to the stars, which he says have made sisters so different from one another. Deferring to the stars effectively absolves Regan and Goneril of any responsibility for their actions and credits fate with determining one sister's virtue and the other's vice. This conversation is important in understanding the role of divine justice in the events that occur later. Albany believes in divine justice, but both Lear and Gloucester have questioned whether such justice exists. The role of fate in understanding God's justice creates some complex issues to consider, since if Kent's words are to be taken literally, Cordelia's death lies with fate and not with divine justice. Divine justice, indeed any concept of God's intervention, cannot co-exist with a reliance on fate to explain events. Of course, it is important to remember that Shakespeare sets his events in the pre-Christian era, while both Shakespeare and his audience exist in a Judeo-Christian world. This creates a paradox and adds to the tension of the text.

Glossary

imports to mean; signify.

smilets small smiles; half-smiles.

question communication; an asking; inquiry.

sovereign above or superior to all others; chief; greatest; supreme.

dog-hearted ferocious; cruel; pitiless.

Act IV
Scene 4

Summary

The setting remains the French camp near Dover. Cordelia is now responsible for leading the French army in its defense of her father. Having learned of her father's deteriorating mental condition, Cordelia quickly sends an officer to search for Lear. She asks the doctor if there is any way the king's mental acuity might be restored and prays that her father's sanity is not lost forever. Within moments, a messenger arrives with news of the English army's arrival, and Cordelia prepares to use the French forces to help defend her father.

Commentary

The opening lines of this scene, which describe Lear's appearance, show how far from his royal state the king has descended. In Act I, Lear assumed the mantel of royalty with accustomed ease, and now he appears covered in weeds. Lear's choice of weeds for raiment, rather than the equally available flowers in the fields, is significant. The king's temperament is as wild and ungoverned as the weeds, which grow so freely, and which represent the unplanned chaotic state of nature.

Royalty should be cautious, planning carefully for the possibility of insurgent "weeds"—or their human equivalents— gaining a foothold in the landscape. Lear's physical self represents the results of the king's unwise abdication of authority and his negligence in tending to his kingdom. Instead of appearing like a carefully designed English garden, Lear and his kingdom show signs of neglect, and both are now infested with a wild outbreak of weeds. Lear, covered in weeds, metaphorically represents the reality of his realm. With the messenger's entrance, Cordelia's role of savior is emphasized. She is present, not as the head of a French invasion, but as a rescuer and defender of her father.

Glossary

rank growing vigorously and coarsely; overly luxuriant.

century a military unit, originally made up of 100 men.

simples a medicinal herb; a medicine made from a plant.

Act IV
Scene 5

Summary

The setting is Gloucester's castle. Oswald reveals to Regan that Albany's forces have been deployed, but with much reluctance. Regan is more interested in the letter that Oswald carries from Goneril to Edmund. Regan insists that the letter be given to her, because she is aware of Goneril's amorous glances toward Edmund. Regan tells Oswald that Edmund is to be reserved for her, since she is now a widow. Regan also directs Oswald to kill Gloucester if he finds him.

Commentary

Albany's reluctance to support his wife's cause is clear as he reluctantly leads his army in defense of the kingdom. Oswald responds to Albany's hesitation by asserting that Goneril is the better soldier, which subordinates Albany's masculinity to his wife's powerful will. Oswald, however, is not accustomed to thinking about the morality of issues. As Goneril's servant, he accepts her orders without question.

Literary Device

Ironically, Regan expresses concern that Gloucester be relieved of his misery, especially since she is directly responsible for that misery. Her "pity of his misery" (IV.5.12) indicates that she is cognizant of public opinion and interested in her subjects' support of her actions. But, Regan does not devote much attention to this consideration; after all, she has already dispatched Edmund to kill his father. Instead, she is concerned with the letter that Oswald is carrying from Goneril to Edmund. Obviously, Regan suspects Goneril of having feelings for Edmund, and the attempts to force Oswald into surrendering the letter lack any subtly. Regan implies that she and Edmund have an understanding, and she hints that their relationship is more than casual.

By the end of this scene, the audience knows that Goneril and Regan are no longer working partners; instead, they have become rivals, engaging in hidden truths and plots. The sisters' competition for Edmund indicates that he is no longer simply the bastard son of Gloucester. Two royal princesses are vying for Edmund's attention, thus legitimizing his new position. At the conclusion of their meeting, Regan, who has already sent Edmund to kill Gloucester, now tells Oswald to kill the old man. She clearly does not want to take a chance that Gloucester might survive to reveal what happened to him.

Glossary

nighted made dark; black.

belike quite likely; probably.

of her bosom have her trust or confidence.

Act IV
Scene 6

Summary

The setting is the country near Dover. Edgar is leading his father to an area, which Edgar assures the suffering earl, is near the cliffs. After Edgar describes the harrowing view of the beach below the cliffs, Gloucester thanks his guide and gives him a jewel as reward for having fulfilled his service. Delivering a final prayer, Gloucester falls forward and loses consciousness. When Gloucester awakens, Edgar easily convinces his father that he has somehow survived the fall from the cliffs and that the poor beggar who was guiding him was really some kind of fiend. According to Edgar, instead of allowing his death, the gods have saved Gloucester. Accepting this explanation, Gloucester vows to be more accepting of the afflictions that he endures.

Lear enters. Gloucester recognizes Lear's voice, whose simple babbling invokes Gloucester's sympathy. Lear's dialogue with Gloucester explores the role of justice, but at its end, the king dissolves into madness.

A Gentleman and attendants arrive, having been sent by Cordelia to find Lear. But the king is frightened and runs from his rescuers. Before he leaves to follow Lear, the Gentleman tells Edgar that the battle is imminent, as both forces are nearby. As Edgar prepares to lead Gloucester to safety, Oswald enters. When he sees Gloucester, Oswald exclaims that Gloucester is the prize he sought and that he will kill the old man. Edgar interferes; the confrontation ends in a fight and Oswald is slain. The dying steward asks Edgar to take his letters to Edmund.

Commentary

Character Insight

Edgar is still disguised as Poor Tom, but he is now better dressed— as a peasant rather than a pitiful soul covered only in a blanket. More importantly, the manner in which he addresses his father indicates compassion, understanding, and an acceptance of his father's flaws. Edgar has forgiven Gloucester, and his voice reflects the sentiment.

Shakespeare signifies the change by having Edgar speak in verse, so the audience is also aware that Edgar is not the same man he was earlier in the play.

Just before he intends to jump, Gloucester acknowledges the strength of the gods, whose justice he earlier questioned, and he prays that Edgar will be blessed. This scene is heart-rendering because Edgar does not reveal his identity. Instead, he permits the deception to continue so that Gloucester can be healed. When Gloucester awakens, he immediately questions if he actually fell, but then quickly resigns himself to his survival. Gloucester then accepts his afflictions and promises to endure until such time as the gods determine that he has suffered long enough.

Theme

Edgar states prior to Gloucester's "fall" that he will not disclose his true identity so that his father might still be cured, but there is ample opportunity after Gloucester awakens to divulge the secret, and yet, Edgar fails to tell Gloucester the truth. Gloucester's ignorance may be necessary for his continuing self-discovery. If Edgar reveals himself in Act IV, Gloucester's opportunities for growth will be cut short, and a major element of the play is the manner in which each character evolves in response to the circumstances that test his/her beliefs, values, and strengths. Gloucester must continue to learn about himself; his movement toward self-truth would be halted if he resolves his conflict with Edgar at this point.

Lear enters once again with the exclamation that "I am the / king himself" (IV.6.83–84). Although he has no kingdom and is no longer the image of a king, the gods made Lear a king and only the gods can revoke his anointed state. When he hears Gloucester's voice, Lear begins a lengthy monologue that reveals all that he has learned since his daughters betrayed him. Lear finally understands that flattery is a hazard to someone in a high position, and thus, he makes sense even in his madness. Lear believed what he knew to be lies because he accepted his older daughters' flattery: "They flattered / me like a dog, and told me I had the white hairs in my / beard ere the black ones were there" (IV.6.96–98).

His understanding of his complicity in the events that followed is a major step in accepting responsibility and in acknowledging that he is not infallible. Lear's words—"Goneril, with a white beard!" (IV.6.96)— might be interpreted as meaning that Lear mistakes Gloucester for Goneril. But more likely, Lear is addressing Goneril and not greeting someone whom he thinks to be Goneril. By portraying her with a white beard, Lear is asserting that his eldest daughter has inverted nature by assuming the authority of her father, and thus, the white beard, which represents knowledge, becomes the guise of his eldest daughter's rule.

Next, Lear moves to a digression on adultery and sexuality, which fits the notion that both Regan and Goneril have fallen victim to excessive desires—something that is closely aligned with excessive sexuality. Thus the reference to Centaurs, which symbolize the complexity of man's intellectual ability joined to the baser desires of animals, accurately describes man's vulnerability to his more animal instincts.

As he continues, Lear moves to another subject: justice. The king has learned that those who profess honesty are often not honest, and even judges can be corrupted and bribed, and so, he advocates a turn to anarchy and a change of the rules of justice. Lear fears that justice cannot or does not exist amid so much dishonesty (IV.6.154–165).

Lear's knowledge that all men must accept their frailty and their humanity parallels Gloucester's own earlier discoveries. Because of his own suffering, Lear has also learned that even he is not above God's justice. At the end of his speech, Lear shifts to a desire for his sons-in-law's deaths, and a clearer picture of his madness emerges. Lear sees himself as a victim of Fortune, a "natural fool of Fortune" (IV.6.189). Finally, consumed with fear, Lear runs away from the Gentleman and attendants who have appeared and are searching for him.

The Gentleman reminds Gloucester and Edgar that Lear has one daughter who is in harmony with nature and who will redeem him from the misery created by Goneril and Regan. His speech also reminds the audience that the battle is drawing near. Lear's appearance and demeanor have shaken Gloucester, and in response, he prays for the gods to save him from despair and promises that he will not try to kill himself again.

Character Insight

Oswald's entrance in this scene results in his death. Although he is warned, he refuses to abandon his orders to murder Gloucester. Oswald is a servant for whom obedience and position are everything. At the beginning of Act IV Scene 2, Oswald was clearly confused that Albany rejected everything that Goneril had accomplished, and here, he expects the peasant who is accompanying Gloucester to simply move out of the way and allow the old man's murder. His sense of obedience is so great that he even asks the man who has killed him to deliver Goneril's letter to Edmund.

Glossary

cock a small boat propelled by oars, esp. one used as a ship's tender.

idle having no value, use, or significance; worthless.

opposeless irresistible.

conceit a flight of imagination; fancy.

bourn a limit; boundary; a domain.

welk'd ridged or twisted.

gauntlet 1. a medieval glove, usually of leather covered with metal plates, worn by knights in armor to protect the hand in combat. 2. **throw down the gauntlet** to challenge, as to combat.

trick a personal habit or mannerism.

fitchew lewd woman; prostitute.

squiny to squint.

benison a blessing; benediction.

ballow a short, thick stick or club.

Act IV
Scene 7

Summary

The scene opens in a tent in the French camp. Cordelia is expressing her gratitude to Kent for the services he has tendered. Within moments, a sleeping Lear is brought into the tent, where Cordelia welcomes him with characteristic gentleness. As his senses return, the confused king asks if he is in France, and Kent assures Lear that he is in his own kingdom. Lear, Cordelia, and the doctor exit, leaving Kent and a Gentleman to discuss the most recent military developments.

Commentary

Cordelia speaks with insight and appreciation when she tells Kent that his goodness is immeasurable. Although Kent's plans are inexplicit and the reason is unclear as to why revealing his identity would interfere with those plans, his devotion to Lear has been evident all along. At the end of this scene, Kent says, "My point and period will be thoroughly wrought / Or well or ill, as this day's battle's fought." (IV.7.96–97).

Kent's destiny is irrevocably connected to that of the king's, with the full meaning of these words manifest in the final scene of the play.

Since his rescue, Lear has been sleeping, and he continues to sleep even as he is brought to Cordelia. When he awakens he thinks he is in hell, having been rescued by an angel:

> You do wrong to take me o'th' grave;
> Thou art a soul in bliss; but I am bound
> Upon a wheel of fire, that mine own tears
> Do scald like molten lead. (IV.7.45–48)

Literary Device

The wheel of fire is a traditional metaphor for hell, deriving from the medieval period. Envisioning hell is not surprising for Lear, since Cordelia has only recently rescued him from a hellish existence on earth.

Character Insight

In the previous scene, Lear related many of the things he has learned during this painful period, but in this brief scene, he clearly shows that he has learned other equally important lessons. In his speech to Cordelia (IV.7.60–69), Lear makes no mention of royalty or of tests to determine the depth of love, as performed in Act I. Lear no longer sees himself as infallible, and he fully expects Cordelia to hate him. When he finally says "I think this lady / To be my child Cordelia" (IV.7.69–70), Lear is finally once again sane.

The music that greets Lear's return to wakefulness signals a return to harmony and replaces the sounds of the storm and the thundering disharmony between Lear and his older daughters. With the inclusion of music, order has returned to Lear's world, as he is reunited with Cordelia. The contrast between Cordelia and her sisters is especially dramatic in this scene. Cordelia has no desire for revenge, nor any need to make her father suffer for having misjudged her. Her virtue and purity make it easy to see why so many critics and scholars described Cordelia as Christ-like or representative of God's goodness.

Glossary

clipp'd inaccurate through omission.

white flakes white hair.

arbitrement an absolute and final decision.

Act V
Scene 1

Summary

Regan, Edmund, and members of their army gather in the British camp near Dover. Regan quizzes Edmund about his feelings for Goneril. Edmund promises Regan that he will not be intimate with her sister.

Goneril and Albany enter. Albany states that he intends to defend the kingdom against the French invaders. Goneril asserts that the fight is not a domestic quarrel, but a defense against an outside enemy.

Edgar, still disguised as Poor Tom, appears and hands Albany the letter he removed from Oswald's body, the letter Goneril wrote ordering Edmund to kill her husband. Edgar leaves, and Edmund enters with news that the opposing forces are near.

Commentary

The opening of this scene reveals that Regan remains very concerned about the relationship between Goneril and Edmund. Regan wants to know the truth or says she does, but she wants to know the truth only if it is what she wants to hear. And so, Edmund obliges with his version of the truth. His relationship to Goneril is only an "honour'd love" (V.1.9). Edmund adopts the language of nobility, just as he has since he first hatched his ambitious plot to rule the kingdom.

Edmund's promise to not form a liaison with a married woman is unconvincing. Certainly, adultery is a sin, but that fact would not stop Edmund, who has demonstrated a propensity for far greater sins. When Goneril enters, her aside indicates how infatuated she, too, is with Edmund. Up to this point, having power has been most important to Goneril; now, quite suddenly, she is willing to lose the battle, and thus the kingdom, rather than lose Edmund. How far her infatuation will extend becomes clear in Scene 3.

Character Insight

As soon as Goneril and Albany enter, he seeks to establish his position regarding the coming battle. Albany's lines demonstrate that he is an honest and just man (V.1.24–27). The king and his supporters are not enemies of the kingdom, but the French invasion is of sufficient purpose to lead his men into battle. Albany's intent is not to treat Lear and his defenders as enemies but only to defend the country against an outside invader. The others agree with Albany to appease him and ensure his cooperation.

The rift between Goneril and Regan becomes more evident, and their competition for Edmund more obvious in this scene. Regan does not trust Goneril and will not allow her to be alone with Edmund, even for a moment. Regan's insistence that Goneril not remain behind with Edmund makes clear how far apart the sisters have moved from their earlier relationship.

In Act I, Goneril and Regan acted as one, both voicing agreement in their flattery of Lear. They again were united in Act II, when they joined together to reduce Lear's forces. But with the inclusion of Edmund into their circle in Act III, they are now completely divided, each mistrusting the other. In turn, Edmund is busy with some plotting of his own. Edmund's growing ambition leads to a hope that Goneril will kill Albany, and in turn, be killed by Regan, who will be free to marry Edmund. With Lear and Cordelia dead, Edmund will be left to rule as king. He has come a long way from the bastard son of Act I.

Glossary

alteration change (of mind).

forfended prohibited; forbidden.

convenient appropriate; suitable.

avouched asserted; affirmed.

greet the time hurry; meet the emergency.

Act V
Scene 2

Summary

The setting is a field between the British and French camps. Cordelia, Lear, and their forces move toward the battle. Edgar enters, looking for a safe place for Gloucester to wait out the conflict. After placing Gloucester in a sheltered spot, Edgar leaves, and the sounds of battle are heard. In a few moments, Edgar returns and orders Gloucester to follow him to a more secure spot because Lear's forces have lost, and the king and Cordelia have been taken prisoner.

Commentary

Theme

Edgar echoes a common belief of Shakespeare's period when he says "Men must endure" (V.2.9). Patient suffering was a key part of seventeenth-century life, a fundamental belief of Christian doctrine. Within this context, the Book of Job was not just a part of the larger biblical text; it was instead, an element of every man's life. Job's trials were thought to be an actual historical account, written by Moses and designed by God to facilitate the acceptance of suffering as necessary for a later reward with God. In short, a belief in patience through suffering created the way to greater happiness and glory with God.

Job's suffering increases with his willingness to suffer; and still, he only responds, "Shall we receive good at the hand of God, and shall we not receive evil?" (Job 2:9). Even when Job can bear his suffering no longer, he refuses to curse God. Instead, he curses the day of his birth. Job's patience with his loss and pain is tremendous, and clearly this serves as a model for Edgar, who has borne his trials with patience. Eventually, even Job begins to question why he must suffer, and in turn, he is chastised by God and reminded of God's glory: "Where were you when I laid the foundation of the earth?" (Job 38:4). The reflective man, willing to suffer, reminded by patience of the reward from God, finds an expression of his glory in Job's text. Although the setting for King Lear is pre-Christianity, its influences are clearly seen in the way Edgar reminds his father that they must endure.

Glossary

good host shelterer, entertainer.

Act V
Scene 3

Summary

The scene opens on the British camp near Dover. Lear and Cordelia are led in as prisoners, with Edmund as their jailer. As the two are led off to prison, Edmund gives a note to an officer and orders that the note's instructions be followed immediately.

Albany, Goneril, and Regan join Edmund. Albany demands that the two prisoners be turned over to him. Edmund resists, saying that Lear and Cordelia will be held in safekeeping so that their presence does not divide the soldiers' loyalty. Albany orders Edmund and Goneril arrested for treason.

Albany requests any man who is willing to support the charges against Edmund to appear. Edgar enters, and although he will not identify himself, he assures Albany that he is as noble as Edmund. With this statement, the brothers begin to fight, and Edmund falls. When Goneril announces that Edmund has been betrayed, Albany reveals the letter, which she does not deny. Instead, Goneril flees.

Edmund admits that the charges against him are truthful. Edgar reveals his identity and tells his brother of recent events, including the news that after disclosing his identity to his father, Gloucester's heart proved too weak to survive the news. Edmund also reports that Kent has been in disguise, having been close enough to help his king during the recent period.

A gentleman enters with news that Goneril has killed herself, but not before poisoning Regan, who is also dead. When Albany discovers Goneril's plan to have both Lear and Cordelia murdered, he quickly orders an officer to intercede, but it is too late. Lear enters with a dead Cordelia in his arms.

Albany recognizes that Lear is king and will be served by his loyal subjects, but within moments, the king dies, his body covering that of his youngest daughter. Albany informs Kent and Edgar that they must now rule the kingdom together, but Kent replies that he will soon leave the world to join his master. Edgar is left to speak of the sad weight of these events, which everyone must now endure.

Commentary

This final scene brings resolution to both the plot and subplot. The scene opens with Lear and Cordelia held prisoner by Edmund. Cordelia's response to their capture evokes the same stoicism exhibited by Edgar and Gloucester: "We are not the first / Who, with best meaning, have incurr'd the worst" (V.3.3–4). While bravely facing these events, Cordelia recognizes they are also at risk. Unlike Cordelia, Lear fails to recognize the danger in which the two captives now find themselves. Lear is merely happy to be with Cordelia, unconcerned that the war is lost and they are prisoners. He is seemingly unaware that they are in danger from Edmund. Lear has only visions of their happiness (V.3.8–15).

Lear asks for nothing more than to be with Cordelia. He will close out the rest of the world and even exclude his oldest daughters. When Cordelia asks if they will see daughters and sisters, Lear's response is a resounding "No, no, no, no!" (V.3.8). His vision of the future excludes all others, except for Cordelia. But Edmund has other plans, as he makes clear after Lear and Cordelia are led to prison. Edmund orders his officer to stage Cordelia's death as a suicide. Without hesitation, the officer accepts Edmund's orders, seemingly unconcerned about killing the king and his daughter. Gaining Edmund's favor will assure the officer continued employment when the war is over. This officer's willingness to kill without question recalls Tyrrel's similar actions in *Richard III*.

Albany has undergone significant change from his initial, docile appearance early in the play. The audience has witnessed his personal growth, and in this scene, the culmination of change is clear when he assumes control following the battle's conclusion. Although he is initially complimentary of Edmund's success in battle, Albany is quickly angered at Edmund's assumption of authority when the illegitimate son has the king and Cordelia arrested and imprisoned.

Albany immediately reminds Edmund that he is a bastard, calling him a "Half-blooded fellow" (V.3.81). Regan's defense of Edmund moves Albany to order Edmund's arrest and to issue a challenge for someone to come forth and fight Edmund. The duel that ensues is quite different from the duel that ends *Hamlet*, which is staged as sport.

Theme

Christian tradition recalls several biblical battles between good and evil, as divine justice is an important component of trial by combat. The duel between Edgar and Edmund is really a conflict that replays this ongoing battle between good and evil, with Edgar's defeat of Edmund obviously signaling the triumph of righteousness over corruption. In the end, Edmund is defeated by being noble, by not being as ruthless as he should be—or was. The system of honor disarms him, and he agrees to a duel, although he recognizes that he does not need to agree to a fight with an unidentified stranger (V.3.140–144).

When fatally wounded, Edmund even adopts the rules of social snobbery claiming, "If thou'rt noble, / I do forgive thee" (V.3.164–165). But unlike Shakespeare's other great villain, Iago, Edmund does repent and tries to rescind his order to execute Cordelia and Lear. In this small measure, he proves himself worthy of Gloucester's blood.

As Albany has earlier prophesized, Goneril and Regan's evil has finally destroyed them. The audience learns early in this scene that Goneril has poisoned Regan (V.3.97), and with Albany's denouncement of Goneril's plotting, Goneril kills herself. Although Gloucester had earlier attempted suicide, ironically only Goneril, who initially appeared so strong, succeeds at ending her own life.

Literary Device

Albany's order to rescue Cordelia and Lear is given too late. When Lear enters with Cordelia's body, any immediate ideas about divine justice are destroyed. The deaths of Cornwall, Edmund, Regan, and Goneril have lulled the audience into a belief that the gods would restore order to this chaotic world. But Cordelia's death creates new questions about the role of divine justice.

Eighteenth-century audiences were disturbed enough by this ending that productions of *King Lear* included a new conclusion, one in which Cordelia lives. But Shakespeare never intended for his audience to escape the painful questions that Cordelia's death creates. The deaths of Gloucester and Lear are acceptable. Both have made serious errors in judgment, and although both came to recognize their complicity in the destruction that they caused, the natural resolution of this change was an acceptance of their future, whatever it held. But Cordelia is young and blameless. She, like Edgar, is completely good and pure. Her death plunges Lear back into madness, as he can find no other way but insanity to deal with such a tragedy.

As is the case in many of Shakespeare's tragedies, at the play's conclusion, the stage is littered with bodies, some deserving of death, and some the innocent victims of evil. Lear lies surrounded with the bodies of his three daughters, just as he was surrounded by them in Act I. Traditionally, the highest ranking individual speaks the last lines in a tragedy, but in this case Edgar is given the final lines, as he responds to Albany's request. Albany, whose rank places him above the rest, has appointed Kent and Edgar to restore order. But Kent intends to follow his master in death, and Edgar's final lines are ambiguous and may portend his own early death. Thus, *King Lear* ends without the clear resolution of many of Shakespeare's other tragedies. Audiences must decide for themselves if divine justice has prevailed.

Glossary

take upon be interested in.

strain ancestry; lineage; descent.

quarrels a cause for dispute.

list a wish; a craving, desire, or inclination.

attaint to prove guilty.

cope to meet, encounter, or have to do (*with*).

maugre in spite of.

descent the lowest point; here, the sole of a shoe.

rings the outer edge or border of something circular; rim, as of a wheel.

tranc'd a stunned condition; daze; stupor.

fordone destroyed, killed, ruined, etc.

CHARACTER ANALYSES

King Lear

Lear is the protagonist, whose willingness to believe his older daughters' empty flattery leads to the deaths of many people. In relying on the test of his daughters' love, Lear demonstrates that he lacks common sense or the ability to detect his older daughters' falseness. Lear cannot recognize Cordelia's honesty amid the flattery, which he craves. The depth of Lear's anger toward Kent, his devoted follower, suggests excessive pride—Lear refuses to be wrong. Hubris leads Lear to make a serious mistake in judgment, while Lear's excessive anger toward Kent also suggests the fragility of his emotional state. Hubris is a Greek term referring to excessive and destructive pride. In the ancient Greek world, hubris often resulted in the death of the tragic, heroic figure. This is clearly the case with Lear, who allows his excessive pride to destroy his family.

Throughout the play, the audience is permitted to see how Lear deals with problems. He is shocked when people do not obey as they have in the past, since Lear is king and he expects to be obeyed. However, instead of dealing with issues, Lear looks to the Fool to distract him with entertainment, to help him forget his problems. He has been insulted and demeaned as king, but he is not prepared to face those who are responsible. Instead, Lear often responds to problems with anger and outbursts of cursing, even a physical attack when provoked. When confronted with insults, Lear is helpless, at the mercy of his daughter and her servants, and he often succumbs to despair and self-pity. The once-omnipotent king struggles to find an effective means of dealing with his loss of power.

Eventually, the king reveals that he is frightened and apprehensive for his future, but he refuses to submit to another's decisions. Lear wants to remain in charge of his destiny, even though the choices he makes are poor or filled with danger. Thus, Lear chooses to go out into the storm because he must retain some element of control. The only other choice is to acquiesce to his daughters' control, and for Lear, that option is not worth considering. Lear is stubborn, like a willful child, and this is just one additional way in which he tries to deal with the events controlling his life. Lear flees into the storm, as a child flees a reality too harsh to accept.

In spite of his despair and self-pity, Lear is revealed as a complex man, one whose punishment far exceeds his foolish errors, and thus, Lear is deserving of the audience's sympathy. Eventually, Lear displays regret, remorse, empathy, and compassion for the poor, a population that Lear has not noticed before. Lear focuses on the parallels he sees to his own life, and so in a real sense, his pity for the poor is also a reflection of the pity he feels for his own situation.

Lear is the anointed king, God's representative, and thus, he shares the responsibility for dispensing justice on earth. He recognizes that he bears responsibility for both his own problems and for those of others, who suffer equally. His understanding of his complicity in the events that followed is a major step in accepting responsibility and in acknowledging that he is not infallible. Because of his own suffering, Lear has also learned that even he is not above God's justice.

Goneril

Goneril is Lear's eldest daughter. After professing her deep love for her father and receiving half of his kingdom, she betrays him and plots his murder. Goneril's expressions of love are extreme and reveal the inherent dishonesty of her nature. Goneril reveals her true character when she defies the hierarchy of nature, which calls for daughters to respect and honor their fathers, and lays the groundwork for the torment she will set in motion for the remainder of her father's life.

Goneril leads her father to believe that her love for him extends beyond any evidence of poor behavior, and so ultimately, she is responsible for Lear's actions, having earlier endorsed them. Later, both Goneril and Regan are depicted as especially cruel and bloodthirsty, as they call for Gloucester's punishment. Throughout most of the play, having power has been most important to Goneril, but by its conclusion, she is willing to lose the battle, and thus the kingdom, rather than lose a man.

Regan

Regan is Lear's second daughter. Regan is as villainous as Goneril. In the beginning, both Regan and Cornwall appear to be conscientious and reasonable people. Regan appears genuinely upset to learn of Edgar's betrayal. Thus, Regan initially appears as the more sympathetic and gentler sister. She greets her father with politeness, but her deportment is deceptive. Regan has no real reverence for her father and king, as her subsequent actions reveal, but Regan is more competent than Goneril at deception, more easily assuming the mantle of deference and politeness that a gracious daughter is expected to exhibit.

Like Goneril, Regan also proves herself to be unyielding and cruel. Regan's plucking of Gloucester's beard reinforces the point that she has no respect for age or rank. In contrast to her basic inhumanity, Regan shows some real humanity, though briefly, when Cornwall is wounded. Regan's concerns that Gloucester should be relieved of his misery indicates that she is cognizant of public opinion and concerned that her subjects support her actions.

Cordelia

Cordelia genuinely loves her father, but her refusal to flatter him leads to the tragedy that unfolds. Cordelia's tears at the news of her father's treatment prove her compassion and establish that she is, indeed, the opposite of her sisters. Cordelia has no desire for revenge, nor any need to make her father suffer for having misjudged her. Her virtue and purity make it easy to see why she is often described as Christ-like or representative of God's goodness. Her response to her father's capture, and her own capture, evokes the stoicism of kings, and reveals that Cordelia is as royal as her father is.

Fool

The Fool assumes the role of Lear's protector when Cordelia is banished. The Fool functions much as a Chorus would in a Greek tragedy, commenting upon events and the king's actions and acting, in some ways, as the king's conscience. The Fool is the king's advocate, loyal and honest, but he is also able to point out the king's faults, as no one else can. The Fool's use of irony, sarcasm, and humor help to ease the truth, and allows him to moderate Lear's behavior. The Fool shares his master's fate, and this reinforces the impression that the Fool's purpose is to protect Lear until Cordelia can arrive to help her father. Both Cordelia and the Fool are caretakers for Lear, and when one is present, the other need not be.

Earl of Gloucester

Gloucester is depicted as a foolish old man, whose inability to see through Edmund's lies parallels Lear's own difficulties. By mistaking Edmund's motives, Gloucester is blind to the events occurring around him, even before Cornwall gouges out his eyes. Clearly, he is not intuitive or quick enough to understand the plotting or undercurrents present around him. Gloucester blames events on the stars, and thus, he absolves himself of any responsibility for his actions.

Later, Gloucester is willing to sacrifice his own life for the king. This heroic behavior sets Gloucester apart from his youngest son, Edmund, who is merely an opportunist. Like Lear, Gloucester feels despair and questions a god, and like Lear, Gloucester finds his humanity in the midst of his tragedy. The blinded old man who asks that clothing be brought, so that Bedlam Tom might be covered, is a very different man from the Gloucester of Act I, who in the play's opening scene, bragged of the good sport to be had at Edmund's conception. Instead of a thoughtless braggart, Gloucester is filled with compassion for Poor Tom. This compassion for his fellow man indicates that Gloucester regrets the behavior of his past, as he seeks to make amends by sharing with those he never noticed before the recent events.

Earl of Kent / Caius

Although banished, Kent disguises himself in an effort to stay close to his king. Kent is honest—he will not lie to his king—and he is truly selfless, devoted to Lear. When his attempts to protect Lear from his own impetuous nature fail, Kent assumes the guise of an ordinary man and resolves to protect his king. When queried by Lear as to his identity, Kent replies that he is "a man" (I.4.10). Thus, he is no one special, and yet, he stands apart from many other men. Kent is a man defined by integrity, whose goodness is immeasurable, as is his love for his king. Kent's destiny is irrevocably connected to that of the king's, as the final scene of the play reveals. In rejecting Albany's offer to rule the kingdom with Edgar, Kent reveals that he will soon join his king in death. Clearly, Kent feels that his job on earth is to serve his king, and with that job now ended, he anticipates his own death.

Edmund

Gloucester's younger illegitimate son is an opportunist, whose ambitions lead him to form a union with Goneril and Regan. The injustice of Edmund's situation fails to justify his subsequent actions. Edmund rejects the laws of state and society in favor of the laws he sees as eminently more practical and useful—the laws of superior cunning and strength.

Edmund's desire to use any means possible to secure his own needs makes him appear initially as a villain without a conscience. But Edmund has some solid economic impetus for his actions, and he acts from a complexity of reasons, many of which are similar to those of Goneril and Regan. To rid himself of his father, Edmund feigns regret and laments that his nature, which is to honor his father, must be subordinate to the loyalty he feels for his country. Thus, Edmund excuses the betrayal of his own father, having willingly and easily left his father vulnerable to Cornwall's anger. Later, Edmund shows no hesitation, nor any concern about killing the king or Cordelia. Yet in the end, Edmund repents and tries to rescind his order to execute Cordelia and Lear, and in this small measure, he does prove himself worthy of Gloucester's blood.

Edgar / Poor Tom

Edgar is Gloucester's only legitimate heir, but he must flee and hide from his father when he comes under suspicion. Edgar's innate honesty and dignity lets him believe that his brother, Edmund, would never lie to him, since Edgar would not lie to his brother. Edgar's stoic belief that he has survived the worst that fortune can throw at him is tested when Edgar discovers his father, now blinded. The manner in which Edgar addresses his father indicates compassion, understanding, and an acceptance of his father's flaws.

Duke of Albany

As Goneril's husband, Albany grows in stature during the play and ultimately finds the strength to resist his wife's efforts to have Lear killed. Early in the play, Albany lacks the strength to stand up to his wife, and thus, he cannot control her. Albany is Goneril's opposite, gentle and kind to his wife's cruel and self-serving demeanor. But later, Albany's attack on Goneril's integrity demonstrates that Albany is a highly moral and humane individual, the antithesis of his wife.

Where Goneril has created chaos, Albany endorses nature's design and a view of nature's work within an organic framework. Albany accepts that nature's pattern is essential for survival. Early on, Albany hesitates to confront Goneril when he thinks she's wrong, but he is not the willing participant in evil that Cornwall is. Albany is genuinely shocked when he learns of Gloucester's blinding, while Cornwall easily succumbs to this depravity.

With a new resistance to his wife, Albany joins the ranks of characters who undergo dramatic change during the course of the play; he grows and evolves into a stronger and more compassionate individual by the end of the drama. Albany leads his army in defense of the kingdom, although with great reluctance. The audience witnesses his personal growth, and the culmination of change is clear when he assumes control of the kingdom following the battle's conclusion.

Duke of Cornwall

Cornwall is Regan's brutal husband, vicious and savage when thwarted in his efforts to seize ambition. Cornwall's easy acceptance of Edmund's story and his welcoming of Edmund into his clique foreshadows the evil that will later emerge from Cornwall and provides a hint to the audience that Cornwall is not what he appears. Cornwall responds to Kent's truthful declarations by placing Kent in the stocks. This action indicates that Cornwall, who himself uses artifice as a substitute for honesty in his own speech, cannot recognize truth when he hears it. Later in the play, Cornwall will make no attempt to control his actions or behave in a civilized manner as he gouges out Gloucester's eyes and grinds them under the heel of his boot.

Oswald

Oswald, Goneril's steward, is a willing accomplice to Goneril's plotting and a henchman without honor. Oswald adds to this negative perception by failing to defend himself against Kent's attack and by lying that he spared Kent's life because Kent is an old man. These events paint Oswald as weak and dishonest. Oswald is, as Kent suggests, a parasite who thrives off Goneril's evil machinations and who makes her deceit easier to maintain. As Goneril's servant, he accepts her orders without question. Although he is warned, he refuses to abandon his orders to murder Gloucester, since obedience and position are everything to this servant. Oswald's sense of obedience is so great that he even asks the man who has killed him to deliver Goneril's letter to Edmund.

King of France

France is honorable and willing to support Cordelia's efforts to rescue her father. France points out that she is a prize as great as any dowry. France's support of Cordelia reveals that he is, indeed, worthy of Cordelia's love.

Duke of Burgundy

Burgundy rejects Cordelia when he discovers that she will bring him no dowry or inheritance. Burgundy, who cannot love Cordelia without her wealth, is guilty of selfish motivations.

CRITICAL ESSAYS

Divine Justice in *King Lear*

King Lear inspires many philosophical questions; chief among them is the existence of divine justice. This concept was particularly important during the Elizabethan era, because religion played such a significant role in everyday life. Religious leaders directed people to expect that they would have to answer to a higher authority, expressing some hope that good would triumph and be rewarded over evil. But throughout *King Lear*, good does not triumph without honorable characters suffering terrible loss. In fact, at the play's conclusion, many of the good characters lie dead on the stage—Lear, Gloucester, and Cordelia. In addition, the audience hears that Kent will soon die, and the Fool has earlier disappeared, presumably to die. Of course, the evil characters are also dead, but their punishment is to be expected according to the laws of divine justice. But how then does the audience account for the punishment and, finally, the death of the good characters in *King Lear?*

Lear makes several poor choices, most importantly in misjudging the sincerity of his daughters' words; but when he flees out into the open heath during a storm, his madness seems a painful and excessive punishment to witness. Parallel to Lear's punishment is that which Gloucester suffers. The plucking of Gloucester's eyes can be perceived as another instance in which divine justice is lacking. Gloucester has made several errors in judgment, as has Lear; but the brutal nature of Gloucester's blinding—the plucking out of his eyes and the crushing of them under Cornwall's boots—is surely in excess of any errors he might have made.

Both Lear and Gloucester endure terrible physical and mental suffering as punishment for their misjudgment, but before dying, both men are reunited with the child each earlier rejected. This resolution of the child-parent conflict, which earlier tore apart both families, may be seen as an element of divine justice, although it offers little gratification for the audience.

Throughout *King Lear*, the audience has witnessed Edmund's growing success as a reward for his evil machinations. But when Edgar and Edmund meet in Act V, the duel between these two brothers is very different from the traditional match for sport. Christian tradition recalls several biblical battles between good and evil, as divine justice is an important component of trial by combat. The duel between Edgar and Edmund is really a conflict that replays this ongoing battle between good and evil, with Edgar's defeat of Edmund obviously signaling the triumph of righteousness over corruption. Edgar's victory, as well as his succession of Lear, as king of Britain, points to an intervention of divine justice.

And yet, when Lear enters with Cordelia's body, any immediate ideas about divine justice vanish. The deaths of Cornwall, Edmund, Regan, and Goneril have lulled the audience into a belief that the gods would restore order to this chaotic world. But Cordelia's death creates new questions about the role of divine justice; a just god could not account for the death of this faithful and loving daughter.

In spite of the seemingly senseless death of this young woman, Shakespeare never intended for his audience to escape the painful questions that Cordelia's death creates. Instead, the audience is expected to struggle with the question of why such tragedies occur. The deaths of Gloucester and Lear are acceptable. Both have made serious errors in judgment, and although both came to recognize their complicity in the destruction that they caused, the natural resolution of this change was an acceptance of their future, whatever it held. But Cordelia is young and blameless. She is completely good and pure.

At the play's conclusion, the stage is littered with bodies, some deserving of death and some the innocent victims of evil. Cornwall has been destroyed by his own honest servant; Edmund is killed by the brother he sought to usurp; both Goneril and Regan are dead, one murdered and the other a suicide; the obedient steward, Oswald, is dead, a victim of his own compulsion to obey. In the end, no easy answer surfaces to the question of divine justice, except that perhaps man must live as if divine justice exists, even if it's only a product of rich and wishful imaginations.

Parent-Child Relationships in *King Lear:* The Neglect of Natural Law

At the heart of *King Lear* lies the relationship between father and child. Central to this filial theme is the conflict between man's law and nature's law. Natural law is synonymous with the moral authority usually associated with divine justice. Those who adhere to the tenets of natural law are those characters in the text who act instinctively for the common good—Kent, Albany, Edgar, and Cordelia.

Eventually, Gloucester and Lear learn the importance of natural law when they recognize that they have violated these basic tenets, with both finally turning to nature to find answers for why their children have betrayed them. Their counterparts, Edmund, Goneril, Regan, and Cornwall, represent the evil that functions in violation of natural law. All four conspirators are without conscience and lack recognition of higher moral authority, since they never consider divine justice as they plot their evil. Their law is man-made, and it focuses on the individual, not the good of the community. Tragedy unfolds as two carefully interwoven and parallel stories explore the abandonment of natural order and the unnatural betrayal of parent and child.

In the primary plot, Lear betrays his youngest daughter and is betrayed by his two oldest daughters. In almost identical fashion, the subplot reveals another father, Gloucester, who betrays his older legitimate son and who is betrayed by his younger illegitimate son. In both cases, the natural filial relationship between father and children is destroyed through a lack of awareness, a renunciation of basic fairness and natural order, and hasty judgment based on emotions. By the play's end, the abandonment of natural order leaves the stage littered with the dead bodies of fathers and their children.

In the opening act, Lear creates a love test to justify giving Cordelia a larger share of his kingdom. Although his kingdom should be divided equally, Lear clearly loves Cordelia more and wants to give her the largest, choice section of his wealth. In return, Lear expects excessive flattery and gushing confessions of love. But instead, Cordelia's reply is tempered, honest, and reasonable—custom dictates that she share her love between her husband and her father.

Just as soon as Cordelia fails to meet her father's expectations, Lear disinherits her. At Cordelia's loss, Goneril and Regan are quick to take advantage. They may have genuinely loved their father at one time, but they now seem tired of having been passed over in favor of their younger sister. After Lear states his obvious preference for Cordelia, the older sisters feel free to seek their revenge, turning the family's natural order on its ear. At the same time, Lear fails to see the strength and justice in natural law, and disinherits his youngest child, thus setting in motion the disaster that follows. Lear puts in place a competition between sisters that will carry them to their graves.

In a similar father-child relationship, the opening scene of *King Lear* positions Gloucester as a thoughtless parent. The audience's introduction to this second father has him speaking of Edmund's birth in a derogatory manner. Although Gloucester says that he loves both

Edmund and Edgar equally, society does not regard the two as equal—and neither does Gloucester, whose love is limited to words and not actions of equality. According to nature's law, Edmund is as much Gloucester's son as Edgar is; but according to man's law of primogeniture, Edmund is not recognized as Gloucester's heir.

In one of the initial pieces of information offered about Edmund, Gloucester tells Kent that Edmund has been away seeking his fortune, but he has now returned. Under English law, Edmund has no fortune at home, nor any entitlement. Edmund's return in search of family fortune provides the first hint that he will seize what English laws will not give him. Clearly, Edmund's actions are a result of his father's preference—both legal and filial—for Edgar, his older and legitimate son. This favoritism leads to Edmund's plan to destroy his father in an attempt to gain legitimacy and Gloucester's estate. Again, the natural order of family is ignored.

Gloucester rejects natural law and a parent's love for his child when he is easily convinced that Edgar—the son he claims to love so much—has betrayed him. Gloucester also puts his faith in Edmund's command of persuasive language, when he rejects the love his eldest son has always shown him. With this move, the earl demonstrates that he can be swayed by eloquence, a man-made construct for easy persuasion, which causes him to reject natural law and the bond between father and child.

Edmund both ignores and embraces natural law. By betraying his father to Cornwall and Regan, Edmund's self-serving course of action abandons nature's order and instead foreshadows the neo-Darwinist argument for survival of the strongest individual. His ability to survive and win is not based on competitive strategies or healthy family relationships; instead, Edmund will take what he desires by deceiving those who trust and love him.

Edmund's greed favors natural law over man's law because natural law doesn't care that Edmund is illegitimate. He claims nature as his ally because he is a "natural" offspring, and because man's law neglects to recognize his rights of inheritance. But, nature only serves Edmund as a convenient excuse for his actions. His actions against his brother and father are more a facet of greed than any reliance on natural law.

One might argue that Gloucester's cavalier attitude toward Edmund's conception mitigates Edmund's actions. When combining this possibility with Edmund's final scene, in which he tries to save Cordelia and Lear, Edmund clearly shows himself to be of different fabric than Goneril, Regan, and Cornwall. In many ways, Gloucester is responsible for what Edmund becomes. Edmund is as much Gloucester's son as is Edgar. In embracing the man-made laws that reject Edmund's legal rights, Gloucester is denying natural laws that would make Edmund and Edgar equal.

Gloucester also acts against nature in rejecting Edgar without sufficient proof of his wrongdoing; thus Gloucester shares responsibility for the actions that follow, just as Lear's love test results in his rejection of Cordelia. Both men are easily fooled and consequently, they both reject natural law and their children. Both act without deliberation, with hasty responses that ultimately betray their descendants.

At the play's conclusion, Goneril and Regan's abandonment of natural order and their subscription to evil has finally destroyed them. The audience learns early in the final scene that Goneril has poisoned Regan and killed herself. Their deaths are a result of unnatural competition, both for power and for love. But Lear is the one who set in motion the need to establish strength through competition, when he pitted sister against sister in the love test.

For the audience, the generational conflict between parent and child is an expected part of life. We grow impatient with our parents and they with us. We attempt to control our children, and they rebel. When Goneril complains that Lear and his men are disruptive and out of control, we can empathize—recognizing that our own parent's visits can extend too long or that our children's friends can be quite noisy. Shakespeare's examination of natural order is central to our own lives, and that is one of the enduring qualities of *King Lear*.

Kingship and Lear

Integrity, compassion, and justice are important facets of an effective king. The king is more than the physical evidence of a strong and united government. The king is God's representative on earth, and as such, serves as a model of behavior for all his subjects, who look to their king for guidance, strength, and hope. If a king lacks the essential components of kingly behavior, and the authority that these traits embody, his subjects will, as Goneril and Regan demonstrate, turn increasingly to deception, treachery, and violence as a method of government. Does Shakespeare's depiction of King Lear offer the audience a portrait of kingship, or in contrast, a portrait of kingly loss?

In his first scene, Lear initially comes across as a strong ruler, although his plan to divide his kingdom among his three daughters seems rather short-sighted and self-serving. This decision places his two strong sons-in-law, Albany and Cornwall, in charge of protecting the outlying areas of the kingdom. But the single benefit derived from this division creates many problems. Lear is abdicating his purpose and his responsibilities, and he is also creating chaos. To achieve his goal, Goneril, Regan, and Cordelia are forced into a love test to determine their inheritance. The division of any kingdom is not without risk, but even before his action has the opportunity to create adversity, Lear establishes a competition, which complicates an already dangerous decision.

Competitions, by their very nature, result in winners and losers. Cordelia loses when she refuses to play the game, but Lear also loses when he "retires" and abdicates his kingly role. He cannot be king without a kingdom, and the country, which is to be divided into smaller principalities, will not have the unity and strength to long survive as separate units. Civil war and insurrection are the inevitable results of Lear's actions. The love test forces Regan and Goneril into competing against the favored younger sister. Ultimately, deadly conflict arises between Lear and his older daughters, and the long-standing competition between sisters creates conflict between ruling factions, further dividing the kingdom.

Even before Cordelia's return, dissent is in the air. In Act II, Curan's report of strife between Albany and Cornwall helps illustrate that Lear's division of his kingdom was a mistake (II.1.10). At this point, conflict doesn't appear to exist between Goneril and Regan, and Cordelia is out of the immediate scene as a result of her banishment. Already, though, Cornwall and Albany show signs of uneasiness, a discord with the clear potential to evolve into conflict, and perhaps, civil war. Goneril and Regan soon unite against a common foe—their own father; but it is reasonable to assume that Goneril and Regan, having disposed of Cordelia, would have next turned their troops and anger against one another. Certainly, Edmund was counting on this event, since he indicates he will marry whichever one survives the struggle for absolute control (V.1.55–69).

Notably, King Lear was not always the ineffectual king represented in the middle and final acts of Shakespeare's play. In the opening of the play, Lear is the absolute ruler, as any king was expected to be in a patriarchal society such as Renaissance England. Lear enters in Act I as the king, evoking grandeur and authority, representing God and the reigning patriarchy of kingship. The audience quickly forgets this initial impression because the love test, in all it absurdity, forces the audience into seeing Lear as a foolish, egotistical old man. But the evidence of his greatness is seen in Kent's devotion, in the love of his Fool, and in Cordelia's love, which is sustained, in spite of Lear's rejection.

By the time Shakespeare was writing *King Lear*, the English had survived centuries of civil war and political upheaval. The English understood that a strong country needed an effective leader to protect it from civil war and potential foreign invasion. The strong leadership of Elizabeth I had saved England when the Spanish attempted an invasion in 1588, and much of the credit for her success was attributed to her earlier efforts to unite England and to end the religious dissention that was destroying the country. No ruler would have deliberately chosen to divide a kingdom, not after having witnessed the conflicts that had marked England's recent history. The division of a country would have weakened it, leading to squabbles between petty lords and the absence of an effective central government and a capable means of defense. Having only recently achieved stability in their country, Shakespeare's Elizabethan audience would have been horrified at Lear's choice to divide his kingdom, and so, create disunity.

The audience would also have questioned the choice of the French king as a suitor, especially as Lear intended to give Cordelia the choice center section of his kingdom. The audience's abject fear that a foreign king might weaken England (and a Catholic monarch made it worse) would have made Lear's actions seem even more irresponsible. But Lear is doing more than creating political and social chaos; he is also giving his daughters complete responsibility for his happiness, and he will blame them later when he is not happy. All of these events create a picture of King Lear as a poor model of kingship, one who reacts emotionally and without reason.

Lear is very much loved by every good character in the play, with only those characters who are unworthy of kingship hating him and plotting against him. Goneril, Regan, Cornwall, and Edmund offer a contrasting image of kingship in their animosity and evil, behavior that is brutal and uncaring, rather than loving and paternal. One other important element of kingship is its connection to natural law and the image of kings as anointed by God. Kingship is directly connected to natural law, which is a central force in this play. A king has absolute authority and has no need to question natural law, and yet kings rule as God's representative on earth; thus their very position creates a recip- rocal agreement between the monarchy and natural law. A successful king works in concert with nature, as Lear does until the moment he disinherits his youngest daughter.

In *King Lear*, the King of France stands as a successful model of how a good and proper king should behave. In his acceptance of Cordelia— even without benefit of a dowry—France is conducting himself with rea- son and conscience. He is also acting within the confines of natural law, with generosity of spirit and a willingness to share his life and country. The model of France's behavior recalls how Lear must have behaved before his decision to divide his land. But instead of seeing this kind father and patriarchal authority, the audience witnesses an absolute ruler, one who refuses questioning, or even the wisdom of his lords. Goneril and Regan equate their share of the land with absolute power of a monarch. They reject any allegiance to God or to any divine justice. Instead, they establish their own system of morality, one based on their father's law rather than natural law. Goneril and Regan can be as absolute in their decisions as Lear chooses to be; their behavior echoes his.

In their choices, Cornwall and Regan remind the audience of Mac- beth and his wife. Cornwall and Regan present a ruling couple,— perhaps even more ruthless, but just as ambitious as the Macbeths— willing to murder their way to absolute power. Goneril and Regan dis- miss Lear's 100 knights, who are really his small personal army. Their action is reasonable if they expect to seize rule and authority. Although the threat of losing a personal guard warrants remedy, Lear's response to this move precipitates the crisis. No king should allow his army to be disbanded, and so Goneril and Regan's actions are certainly danger- ous to the king. But by this time, Lear has waited too late to reclaim the kingship that he has denied.

At the conclusion of the play, Albany appoints Kent and Edgar to restore order, although Albany's rank places him above the other two. But Kent intends to follow his master in death and that leaves Edgar to inherit the kingdom. In spite of the recent events, Albany thinks that Kent and Edgar can rule jointly, but Kent is correct in choosing another future for himself.

Although traditionally, the highest-ranking individual speaks the last lines in a tragedy, Shakespeare gives Edgar the final lines, as Glouces- ter's surviving son responds to Albany's request. Edgar is clearly uncer- tain and reluctant to assume the crown. Kingship was never his goal, nor his intent. But circumstances have forced him to consider a position for which he is unprepared.

Shakespeare has not offered the audience much to appreciate about Edgar. For much of the play, Edgar was disguised as Poor Tom, and the audience saw only a poor creature from Bedlam. Edgar really steps forward when he challenges Edmund, revealing that he has the goodness and strength to defeat evil. In winning their duel, Edgar's defeat of Edmund signals the triumph of righteousness over corruption and provides an assurance of God's blessing on Edgar. This act signals his ability to assume the role of king. In Edgar, kingship is exemplified by integrity, compassion, and justice—all the elements that Lear once possessed but which were subordinated to his injured ego.

CliffsNotes Review

Use this CliffsNotes Review to test your understanding of the original text and reinforce what you've learned in this play. After you work through the review and essay questions, identify the quote section, and the fun and useful practice projects, you're well on your way to understanding a comprehensive and meaningful interpretation of Shakespeare's *King Lear.*

Q&A

1. The conversation between Kent and Gloucester that opens the play serves what purpose?

   a. To reveal that Gloucester liked Edmund's mother.

   b. To give the reader or audience a chance to know Kent before he returns in disguise.

   c. To establish that Edmund is entitled to inherit Gloucester's estate and title.

2. Why is Lear so angry with Cordelia when she refuses to flatter him during the love test?

   a. He wants a reason to give her the best share of his kingdom and excessive protestations of love would justify such a move.

   b. He is an old man who wants to be reassured that all of his children love him unconditionally and boundlessly.

   c. He does not want Cordelia to marry and leave him.

3. Why does Goneril give Oswald a letter for Edmund?

   a. She wants a secret meeting with Edmund.

   b. She wants Edmund to kill her husband.

   c. She asks Edmund to marry Regan.

4. Why does Edmund agree to a duel with the disguised Edgar?

   a. He needs to win to escape from Albany.

   b. He is supremely confident of his ability to beat anyone.

   c. He does not know that rules of conduct prohibit his dueling with a commoner.

5. Why does Kent decline Albany's request to restore order to the kingdom?

    a. He expects to join Lear in death.

    b. He has no desire to take on the problems of ruling a country.

    c. He thinks that two men cannot rule effectively.

Answers: (1) b. (2) a. (3) b. (4) b. (5) a.

Identify the Quote

1. I grow; I prosper;/Now, gods, stand up for bastards.

2. You have begot me, bred me, loved me: I/Return those duties back as are right fit,/Obey you, love you, and most honour you.

3. Blow, winds, and crack your cheeks! rage! blow!/You cataracts and hurricanoes, spout/Till you have drench'd our steeples, drown'd the cocks!

Answers: (1) The speaker is Edmund in Act I, Scene 2. Edmund's opening soliloquy establishes his true character. (2) The speaker is Cordelia in Act I, Scene 1. Cordelia's reply to her father reveals the natural bond between child and father. (3) The speaker is Lear in Act III, Scene 2. Lear rages against the actions of his daughters as the Fool listens.

Essay Questions

1. Examine the specific ways that Lear contributes to his fall.

2. A tragic hero moves the reader to pity, since his misfortune is greater than he deserves, and he also creates fear, since his tragedy might easily befall one of us. To what extent does Lear fit the definition of a tragic hero?

3. Discuss either Lear or Gloucester's movement toward a greater knowledge of himself and his world.

4. The play raises important questions about divine justice. All those who are evil are dead, but so are several of the characters who represent good. Does God see to it that good people are rewarded and evildoers are punished? Write an essay that responds to the question of whether or not divine justice is served in this play.

5. Focus on the repetition of several words, such as nothing, bond, nature, and natural. Choose two of these words and discuss the ideas that their use suggests.

Practice Projects

1. Design a character genealogy chart that demonstrates why Edgar will be king when Lear dies.

2. Construct a chart that compares the characteristics of a king. On one side, list the requirements that Machiavelli gives in *The Prince*. On the other side, list Lear's characteristics.

3. Shakespeare's plays are meant to be heard, not just read. Thus, the plays are more easily understood if studied in performance. Selecting a seemingly difficult scene to present to an audience will add depth to your understanding of the text and make complex characters easier to grasp. For instance, the Fool's speech makes his character difficult for readers to understand and appreciate. To make the Fool's words clearer through performance, ask fellow students to help prepare Act III, Scene 2 to present to your classmates.

CliffsNotes Resource Center

The learning doesn't need to stop here. CliffsNotes Resource Center shows you the best of the best— links to great information in print and online about William Shakespeare and *King Lear*. And don't think that this is all we've prepared for you; we've put all kinds of pertinent information at www.cliffsnotes.com. Look for all the terrific resources at your favorite bookstore or local library and on the Internet. When you're online, make your first stop www.cliffsnotes.com, where you can find more incredibly useful information about the playwright and his works.

Books

This CliffsNotes book provides a meaningful interpretation of the play, *King Lear*. If you are looking for information about the author and/or related works, check out these other publications:

Shakespeare: The Invention of the Human, by Harold Bloom, focuses on Shakespeare's major plays, arguing that much of what mankind thinks about humanity is derived from Shakespeare's plays. There are separate chapters on each of the plays. New York: Riverhead Books, 1998.

Shakespeare the Movie: Popularizing the Plays on Film, TV, and Video, edited by Lynda Boose and Richard Burt, is a collection of essays that explores the impact of the media on the study of Shakespeare. The essays contained in this collection examine the intersection of culture, literary criticism, and the literary canon. London: Routledge, 1997.

The Norton Shakespeare: Based on the Oxford Edition, edited by Stephen Greenblatt, et al., contains all of Shakespeare's plays and poetry, arranged in chronological order. Each work is preceded by a careful discussion of the text, including sources and textual history. There is also extensive information about Shakespeare's life and the time in which he was writing. New York: W.W. Norton, 1997.

King Lear: New Casebooks, edited by Kiernan Ryan, examines the changes in the way critics view *King Lear*. Kiernan explores several of the important debates evolving from recent criticism of the play. New York: St. Martin's Press, 1992.

Women Reading Shakespeare, 1600–1900: An Anthology of Criticism, edited by Ann Thompson and Sasha Roberts, offers a comprehensive look at how Shakespeare has informed women's writing. Since Shakespeare's work first appeared, women have been writing in response to issues and ideas derived from the plays. Roberts includes many texts that are not generally available to readers, and thus, she provides a glimpse into the way early women writers were able to appropriate Shakespeare to meet their own needs. New York: St. Martin's Press, 1997.

Shakespeare in the Theatre: An Anthology of Criticism, compiled by Stanley Wells, is a collection of eyewitness accounts of the performances of Shakespeare's plays from the seventeenth century to the present. Many of the early reviews are not generally available, but their accounts of the plays reveal how the staging of the plays responded to the period and location of the production. London: Oxford University Press, 1997.

Internet

Check out these Web resources for more information about William Shakespeare and *King Lear:*

Web Resources For William Shakespeare's *King Lear,* `http://king lear.rutgers.edu/index-welcome.html`—This site offers links to full texts, sources, criticism, films, and art. Information is easy to find and useful.

Arden Net, `www.ardenshakespeare.com/main/welcome.html`— This site offers texts, resources, and general information about Shakespeare. This very useful resource includes a review of Internet sites, a listing of professional organizations, essays on teaching, and lists of performances. Registration is free.

ELF Presents The Plays of William Shakespeare, `www.the plays.org/`—This site includes texts of plays, character guides, a glossary, and a chronology. Each play also includes a concordance, quotes, and a search engine.

Shakespeare's Globe, `http://shakespeares-globe.org/IE-home. htm`—This site includes information about the reconstruction of the Globe theatre in London. It includes a virtual tour and photographs. There is also information about performances and tickets and what to do when visiting.

Best Sites, `http://daphne.palomar.edu/shakespeare/best sites.htm`—This site is considered to be among the better sites devoted to Shakespeare. It includes criticism, a biography, sources, and general historical information. Also included are links to other sites.

Films

Check out these film adaptations of *King Lear:*

Peter Brook, director. *King Lear.* Royal Shakespeare Company, 1971. This production of King Lear is an updated version of the play, with powerful performances to recommend it.

Jonathan Miller, director. *King Lear.* British Broadcasting Company, 1982. This film was made for television, and is also known as the BBC Television *King Lear.*

Michael Elliott, director. *King Lear.* Granada Television, 1984. This film was made for television, and stars Sir Lawrence Olivier as Lear. This is one of Olivier's final performances.

Richard Eyre, director. *King Lear.* British Broadcasting Company, 1997. This is a National Theatre production of *King Lear* that has been restaged for television. Reviews of the stage production were very favorable, and the film is considered one of the best productions of this play.

Akira Kurosawa, director. *Ran.* Herald Films, 1985. This film is a Japanese adaptation of *King Lear*, and is widely considered to be an excellent production of the play. Instead of daughters, who betray him, Lear has sons.

Journals

Subscribe to these journals for more information on William Shakespeare and *King Lear:*

The Department of English at Iona College in New Rochelle, New York publishes *The Shakespeare Newsletter* four times a year. Subscriptions are $12 per year. This useful newsletter provides information about Shakespeare Summer Festivals and performances of Shakespeare's works. The newsletter also contains articles, which focus on plays and performances and recent Shakespearean criticism. *The Shakespeare Newsletter* is published by the Department of English,

Iona College, New Rochelle, NY 10801. Call (914) 633-2061 to subscribe.

Shakespeare Magazine is directed toward teachers and students but is of interest to anyone who loves Shakespeare. Typical issues contain interviews, photos, and discussion of upcoming productions and films, as well as articles of interest about Shakespeare's texts. Subscriptions are $12 per year. To subscribe, write to Georgetown University, P.O. Box 571006, Washington, DC 20057-1006.

Send Us Your Favorite Tips

In your quest for learning, have you ever experienced that sublime moment when you figure out a trick that saves time or trouble? Perhaps you realized that you were taking ten steps to accomplish something that could have taken two, or you found a little-known workaround that gets great results. If you've discovered a useful tip that helped you understand *King Lear* or other Shakespearean plays and you'd like to share it, the CliffsNotes staff would love to hear from you. Go to our Web site at www.cliffsnotes.com and click the Talk to Us button. If we select your tip, we may publish it as part of CliffsNote-A-Day, our exciting, free e-mail newsletter. To find out more or to subscribe to a newsletter, go to www.cliffsnotes.com on the Web.

Index

CliffsNotes
@ cliffsnotes.com

CliffsNotes

LITERATURE NOTES

Absalom, Absalom!
The Aeneid
Agamemnon
Alice in Wonderland
All the King's Men
All the Pretty Horses
All Quiet on the
  Western Front
All's Well &
  Merry Wives
American Poets of the
  20th Century
American Tragedy
Animal Farm
Anna Karenina
Anthem
Antony and Cleopatra
Aristotle's Ethics
As I Lay Dying
The Assistant
As You Like It
Atlas Shrugged
Autobiography of
  Ben Franklin
Autobiography of
  Malcolm X
The Awakening
Babbit
Bartleby & Benito
  Cereno
The Bean Trees
The Bear
The Bell Jar
Beloved
Beowulf
The Bible
Billy Budd & Typee
Black Boy
Black Like Me
Bleak House
Bless Me, Ultima
The Bluest Eye & Sula
Brave New World
The Brothers Karamazov

The Call of the Wild &
  White Fang
Candide
The Canterbury Tales
Catch-22
Catcher in the Rye
The Chosen
The Color Purple
Comedy of Errors…
Connecticut Yankee
The Contender
The Count of
  Monte Cristo
Crime and Punishment
The Crucible
Cry, the Beloved
  Country
Cyrano de Bergerac
Daisy Miller &
  Turn…Screw
David Copperfield
Death of a Salesman
The Deerslayer
Diary of Anne Frank
Divine Comedy-I.
  Inferno
Divine Comedy-II.
  Purgatorio
Divine Comedy-III.
  Paradiso
Doctor Faustus
Dr. Jekyll and Mr. Hyde
Don Juan
Don Quixote
Dracula
Electra & Medea
Emerson's Essays
Emily Dickinson Poems
Emma
Ethan Frome
The Faerie Queene
Fahrenheit 451
Far from the Madding
  Crowd
A Farewell to Arms
Farewell to Manzanar
Fathers and Sons
Faulkner's Short Stories

Faust Pt. I & Pt. II
The Federalist
Flowers for Algernon
For Whom the Bell Tolls
The Fountainhead
Frankenstein
The French
  Lieutenant's Woman
The Giver
Glass Menagerie &
  Streetcar
Go Down, Moses
The Good Earth
The Grapes of Wrath
Great Expectations
The Great Gatsby
Greek Classics
Gulliver's Travels
Hamlet
The Handmaid's Tale
Hard Times
Heart of Darkness &
  Secret Sharer
Hemingway's
  Short Stories
Henry IV Part 1
Henry IV Part 2
Henry V
House Made of Dawn
The House of the
  Seven Gables
Huckleberry Finn
I Know Why the
  Caged Bird Sings
Ibsen's Plays I
Ibsen's Plays II
The Idiot
Idylls of the King
The Iliad
Incidents in the Life of
  a Slave Girl
Inherit the Wind
Invisible Man
Ivanhoe
Jane Eyre
Joseph Andrews
The Joy Luck Club
Jude the Obscure

Julius Caesar
The Jungle
Kafka's Short Stories
Keats & Shelley
The Killer Angels
King Lear
The Kitchen God's Wife
The Last of the
  Mohicans
Le Morte d'Arthur
Leaves of Grass
Les Miserables
A Lesson Before Dying
Light in August
The Light in the Forest
Lord Jim
Lord of the Flies
The Lord of the Rings
Lost Horizon
Lysistrata & Other
  Comedies
Macbeth
Madame Bovary
Main Street
The Mayor of
  Casterbridge
Measure for Measure
The Merchant
  of Venice
Middlemarch
A Midsummer Night's
  Dream
The Mill on the Floss
Moby-Dick
Moll Flanders
Mrs. Dalloway
Much Ado About
  Nothing
My Ántonia
Mythology
Narr. …Frederick
  Douglass
Native Son
New Testament
Night
1984
Notes from the
  Underground

CliffsNotes™
@ cliffsnotes.com

Check Out the All-New CliffsNotes Guides

TECHNOLOGY TOPICS

Balancing Your Check-
book with Quicken
Buying and Selling
on eBay
Buying Your First PC
Creating a Winning
PowerPoint 2000
Presentation
Creating Web Pages
with HTML
Creating Your First
Web Page
Exploring the World
with Yahoo!
Getting on the Internet
Going Online with AOL
Making Windows 98
Work for You

Setting Up a
Windows 98
Home Network
Shopping Online Safely
Upgrading and
Repairing Your PC
Using Your First iMac
Using Your First PC
Writing Your First
Computer Program

PERSONAL FINANCE TOPICS

Budgeting & Saving
Your Money
Getting a Loan
Getting Out of Debt
Investing for the
First Time
Investing in
401(k) Plans
Investing in IRAs
Investing in
Mutual Funds
Investing in the
Stock Market
Managing Your Money
Planning Your
Retirement
Understanding
Health Insurance
Understanding
Life Insurance

CAREER TOPICS

Delivering a Winning
Job Interview
Finding a Job
on the Web
Getting a Job
Writing a Great Resume